FINDING MY FEET

MY AUTOBIOGRAPHY

FINDING MY FEET

MY AUTOBIOGRAPHY

JASON ROBINSON

with Malcolm Folley

Hodder & Stoughton

Copyright © 2003 Jason Robinson

First published in Great Britain in 2003
by Hodder and Stoughton
A division of Hodder Headline

The right of Jason Robinson to be identified as the Author of
the Work has been asserted by him in accordance with the
Copyright, Designs and Patents Act 1988.

6 8 10 9 7

A CIP catalogue record for this title
is available from the British Library

ISBN 0 340 82655 X

Typeset in Plantin by Palimpsest Book Production Limited,
Polmont, Stirlingshire
Printed and bound in Great Britain by
Mackays of Chatham plc, Chatham, Kent

Hodder and Stoughton
A division of Hodder Headline
338 Euston Road
London NW1 3BH

Photographic Acknowledgements

The author and publisher would like to thank the following for
permission to reproduce photographs:

Altered Images Photography, Colorsport, Getty Images/Allsport, Phill
Heywood, Clint Hughes, Hunslet Club for Boys and Girls/Daniel Webb,
Hunslet Parkside Rugby League Club/Colin Cooper, Lancashire Publications
Ltd, Landrover, manchester Evening News, Marks & Spencer, Mirrorpix,
News International/The Times, Mark Pain, Popperfoto.com, Press
Association, Rugby Times Weekly Newspaper/Rugby League World
Magazine, Sale & Altrincham Messenger, Sale Sharks Rugby Union Football
Club, Tissot, Simon Wilkinson Photography.

All other photographs are from private collections.

CONTENTS

I dedicate this book to Amanda,
who has blessed me with a love that I never knew existed.
She has supported me through good times and bad,
and unselfishly she gave up her career to devote her life
to me, our children and, above all, to God.

ACKNOWLEDGEMENTS

I wish to thank Amanda and the children for helping me to bring this book together; Amanda's parents, Lynne and David, without whose love and understanding this story may never have been written; my mum Dorothy and brothers Bernard and George, for their unconditional love and support over the years.

In no particular order, I also have to thank Danny Webb and all at Hunslet Boys Club for encouraging me to play the game that gave me an inner confidence to carry through life; Colin and Una Cooper, the backbone of Hunslet Parkside Amateur Rugby League Football Club, and all those who dedicated their time to assisting at the club; good friends Mary and Eric Hawley, the man who helped realise my dream; John and Julie Monie, whose assistance on and off the field has helped to make me the player I am today. From Wigan Rugby Club, I am grateful to Graeme West, Keith Mills, Mary Sharkey, Mandy Johnson, Andy Pinkerton, Maurice Lindsay, Jack Robinson, John Martin and the many great players I have had the pleasure of playing alongside. I am indebted to Va'aiga Tuigamala for showing me by the way he lived what Christianity was in the flesh; Daphne Tuigamala and Apollo and Selina Perelini, John and Anne Strickland, Alex Robertson, Geoff Bates, Cath Ashcroft and many more Christian brothers and sisters whose friendship and guidance have been invaluable; Maurice and Joanna Barratt for the Biblical teaching, support and great friendship; and Malcolm Norris. I am thankful to Dave Swanton, my right-hand man, who is appreciated more than he will ever know, and for the work of his son, Dan. I will never forget Peter Deakin, who, sadly, passed away while this book was being written. A big thanks, too, to Sian, Clifford, Abi, Laura and all at Octagon, whose professionalism, encouragement and advice, has enabled me to fulfil my potential away from the playing field. I am grateful to Brian Kennedy for making me share his vision for Sale Sharks, where Ian Blackhurst, Jim Mallinder and Steve Diamond have given me unwavering assistance; and to the management of the England rugby team for their belief: Clive Woodward, Andy Robinson, Phil Larder, Dave Alred, Dave Reddin, Phil Keith-Roche, Simon Hardy and all the backroom staff behind them, and to Jane Woodward for her kindness. I am aware of the support I have received from the stands and from sponsors alike; thank you.

I'd like to thank Malcolm Folley, Chief Sports Reporter for the *Mail on Sunday*, for his time, patience, commitment and, most of all, his friendship; without his contribution this book would not have been written. His wife Rachel, and teenaged daughters, Sian and Megan, also deserve recognition for uncomplainingly allowing Malcolm to spend an inordinate amount of time in my company over the winter and spring. Last but not least, I am also appreciative of the efforts of Roddy Bloomfield, consultant editor at Hodder & Stoughton, not once did he moan, no matter what late changes were passed by his desk.

FOREWORD

Jason was the one taking the risk, not me, when I asked him
to consider switching from rugby league to rugby union towards
the end of 1999; but from the moment we met I sensed he was
eager for a new challenge. After all, in almost ten years with
Wigan, where he was a superstar, he had achieved everything
he could and he had won all there was to win.

Jason's professionalism was evident from the first session he
attended with the England squad. You could see his presence
added a spark to training. All the established England players
were massively interested to see what he was going to be like.
At his first team meeting, he studiously took notes. I was
watching Jason because the other players were watching him.
Whatever time training was scheduled to start, Jason would be
out fifteen minutes before everyone else to get his preparation
right. He was setting examples for us all – and you can't overstress this. Ostensibly, the game of rugby union was amateur
until 1997 and Jason had been a professional player for years
longer than anyone else in the squad.

From the beginning, he showed himself to be an incredibly
modest man. When you read his life story, it is apparent that
he had to overcome huge disadvantages to make his mark as
an international sportsman. He is also candid enough to admit
to mistakes he made. Yet Jason has survived all the bumps and

bruises life threw his way to become an impeccable role model, on and off the field. He is a superb team player, in all senses. He is a devoted father and husband and a devout Christian. He also has a mischievous sense of humour.

When he was selected to tour Australia with the British and Irish Lions in 2000 – before he had started a game for England – I was selfishly delighted from England's point of view. It was a chance for his game to develop further and it was exposing him to the game at the highest level. After he scored the opening Lions try in the First Test in Brisbane, it was one of those moments when you just jump to your feet and go potty! It was pure brilliance from Jason against arguably the best defensive team in the world.

My passion for rugby league developed when I went to live in Australia in 1985. I stayed for five years and saw so many world-class players that I grew to appreciate what a great game it is. When I was appointed England coach in 1997, I realised that I had an opportunity to make groundbreaking changes. I had hoped that I might be able to recruit some of the leading rugby league players to the England team in time for the 1999 Rugby World Cup, and Jason was one of the men I wanted even then. One on one, he has few rivals.

In reality, the turbulent political climate that enveloped rugby union in the infancy of the game turning professional meant I had to be patient longer than I thought, but the wait was worthwhile. Jason's impact has been all – and more – than I could have dared hope and we anticipate him playing an important role at the Rugby World Cup 2003.

Clive Woodward
England Head Coach

1

HOME TRUTH

'He heals the broken hearted and binds up their wounds.'

PSALM 147:3

I used to hate weekends. I never knew when our little terraced house in Beeston, an inner-city suburb of Leeds, was going to be turned into a battleground. Watching your mum being beaten up is something no one should have to experience. It is hard to describe how painful that is, how awful it is to be unable to do anything about it. It was also terrifying.

There was bloodshed and screaming rows in that house at 58 Ingleton Street – not all the time, but often enough to make it not unusual. An air of menace pervaded the house, but I arrived at a point where I became so numbed by the dreadful events that I supposed everyone lived like that. Plates and glasses flew in anger. On one occasion the television was hurled through a window into the street. I was the little kid in the corner, forgotten and ignored, a witness that no one noticed when the fists were flying. I was utterly helpless and I was scared. Alcohol was the catalyst, the reason why sometimes weekends were to be feared.

I should explain that my mum provided a great deal of love

for my two older half-brothers, Bernard and George, and me; she just wasn't brilliant at choosing men. Although my step-father, Richard Robinson, provided me with some happy child-hood memories in moments of sober kindness – he certainly supported my love of rugby – it was his violent, unremitting rage in drink that stained so much of my boyhood without me realising it until recently.

Our house had a living room and kitchen, a bedroom and bathroom upstairs, and two more bedrooms in what originally had been the loft. It also had a cellar. It was just up the street from the Rowland Road Working Men's Club where Richard and my mum would go on Friday and Saturday evenings to play bingo or watch some entertainment; and to drink.

On some weekends, I'd be taken along as well. I'd get dressed up in my smartest clothes – mostly hand-me-downs from George who is four years older than me and who, from an early age, liked to be trendy. Sometimes, I'd wear a tie, which was kind of comical when I think back. I would get to play bingo with old stubs. If I won, Mum would give me 10p for a correct line or 20p for a 'house'. Later, some band would play. This was Mum and Richard's social life, the big night out at the end of a hard working week with so little reward in their pay packets. It never seemed to take much to ignite a row when they got home.

When I didn't go to the working men's club at the weekend, I was left by myself watching television. If one of my brothers came in, he might turn on me, whether I said anything cheeky or not. Invariably, he would have had more than a few beers. One night, one of them scared me so much – and it really doesn't matter which one it was – that I went outside and sat on a wall in the pitch dark. I was too afraid to go back into the house until someone else in the family came home. My other brother came down the street and found me. We went into the house together, and they ended up fighting.

It was not an infrequent pattern. One would be nasty to me, the other would stick up for me and they would go at one another; not wrestling, proper stuff. Drink had the better of both of them, so the smallest incident was enough excuse for a fight. Neither would ever back down, and they tore into one another as though they were battling their worst enemy. Often, they would make one another bleed. I was scared by their ferocity.

If it was not Bernard and George fighting, or Richard and my mum, it would be Richard and one of the boys. The worst, though, was anything that involved my mum. She is a small, fiercely proud and hard-working woman from Scotland. Seeing her being beaten broke my heart. No one deserved the hard time she had. I can remember jumping on Richard's back, trying to drag him off but being too small to be effective. My brothers would also try to stop him, but for a long time they couldn't hurt or discourage him. I can remember ringing the police, and I vividly recall George screaming at Richard one night, 'When I'm older I'm going to kill you.' It's hard to admit that I was consumed by the same dark thoughts because no one likes to release such skeletons from the cupboard.

I don't want to give the impression that a fight erupted in our house every weekend. I have come to understand that the human condition is selective when it comes to preserving our memories. But at the same time, I remember crying at what I had to watch. I don't think the boys realised how bad they were.

Of course, I didn't know who was wrong or who was right. It didn't seen to matter. I saw and heard so much, the bloody violence, the obscene rows, and for years I tried to pretend that it had not happened.

We all endure ups and downs in life, but this was at the extreme end of the spectrum. I am still a bit numb from it all, if I am honest, but by being open, I am trying to offer comfort and hope to the untold numbers of children still having to live through the horror of domestic violence.

I am proud of being from a working-class family, and I hope that others can take inspiration from the fact that I started my journey through life with little more than a mother's love. Her own childhood was not easy, yet no less loving. She told me one day, 'My dad was a miner and my mum was sick. I remember seeing her through a hospital window. We never really had a mum. My dad brought up six children. The only thing we had was happiness.'

Hope is something none of us can be denied. If I am seen to have excelled at the game of rugby, it is because I followed a dream. I am proof that if you put your heart, your mind and time into something, you can achieve what you want.

Academically, I failed. If I could turn back the clock, I'd try a lot harder at school, and certainly I am encouraging my children to concentrate on their education.

Most people look at me now and see only glamour – a big house, a loving family, cars, sponsorship deals, an enviable salary. They create an identikit portrait in their mind – but it is not a picture of the real me. Once I helped my mum clean toilets, now I employ a cleaner of my own. Once I could not afford trainers, now I am paid to wear Puma's latest shoes and boots. I am invited to mix with millionaires, but I know how hard it is for kids being brought up in one-parent families. I know about drugs through the desperate struggles of my brother George. I know what heartache they can cause and how they can ruin lives. I know about domestic violence. I've been there.

Over the years, I have also experienced trials of my own. I have drunk myself into an abyss. I thought about taking my own life. I have made countless mistakes.

When you haven't got money, you think money is the answer. You believe it will bring happiness. You believe it will bring your kids toys that you can't afford. You believe it will get you that holiday you always wanted. You know it will stop you worrying about having the electric or the gas cut off. Then, you get money and with it you get other problems. Who do you trust? Who are your friends, real friends and not those drawn to you because you have sudden wealth? Is it me they like, or is it what I can buy for them that makes me a friend? Money makes life easier for a while, but you are simply introduced to other complications. Money can buy you material things – the flash car, the bright lights, and, believe me, I have invested heavily in all such luxuries – but it is not the answer to being happy. Many wealthy people are miserable.

I suppose the biggest thing for me in all this is having accepted the Lord into my life. I hope I can see all the vagaries of wealth and poverty for what they are. Of course, it makes it easier to be able to provide for my family and I admit it makes me feel better if I can give them everything they want. But you can make a lot of mistakes and a lot of foolish decisions by having money. Knowing what is and what isn't important is the key to striking the balance – more easily said than done. I really don't know how I could go on, day to day, without knowing that God is with me in all I do. I dread to think where I might be otherwise – dead, even.

This is why I have come to have some understanding for Richard Robinson, and the pain, anguish, hurt and bruises he caused us all, but mostly my mum. Without being too judgemental on others, first you must look at your own life. I have failed in so many areas and continue to do so, but not in as many areas as I once did. Life is hard, really hard. Without God, I'd end up slipping back, going back into the pubs and clubs. There's still some of the old me there, the undesirable young man who drank to wild excess to escape from the problems of his own creation.

I have to put some things to rest. Once I felt anger for Richard, now it's more a feeling of curiosity. I want to know why he acted as he did. What did he go through as a child or young man? What horrors did he know, what deep scars has he got? Or was it simply the behaviour of someone reacting to alcohol?

Back in those days in Ingleton Street, there was no time for such reflection. There was only the fear and loathing of what would happen next. Who would be bloodily rebuked for daring to be in the same house after he came home from the Rowland Road Working Men's Club with a skinful?

In the manner of all bullies, Richard met his match one night. Just as he had promised, George became strong enough to stand up to him. I watched as George cornered him on the landing and beat him up, just as Richard had beaten Mum. Richard had no answer to those punches; they hurt him and cut him down. It felt like I was fighting him myself. Richard got up, walked unsteadily downstairs and out through the door. Not long afterwards, he was out of our lives for good.

I cannot tell you how happy I was.

2
WHAT'S IN A NAME?

'In any moment of decision the best you can do is the right thing – the worst you can do is nothing.'

THEODORE ROOSEVELT

I have never met my father. He could be dead for all I know. My mum did point him out one day when we were in Leeds, but that was a long, long time ago. All I know about him is that he is Jamaican and his name is William Thorpe.

Originally, I was called Jason Thorpe Brannan because my mum had kept her married name although she was divorced from her husband, George Brannan. I don't recall her talking about my dad, and I have no feelings towards him. If he had wanted to find me, he could have done. Maybe he felt that would not have been the right thing to do. After all, he washed his hands of me from the beginning. My wife Amanda is more curious about him and what kind of man he is than I am. I think she would like to know if I bear any resemblance to him.

For much of my childhood, Mum played the role of mother and father. As a parent, I know how hard it is to be just one of those, but I didn't think much about it when I was growing up. Kids are not overly sensitive about these matters, are they?

Where we lived, a lot of women were bringing up children on their own. In recent years, though, I have begun to appreciate how wretched a time Mum had, bringing up three boys by herself most of the time. Life has hardened her. She is very introverted and doesn't easily show her feelings.

I have a similar personality, shy by nature, although I am more outgoing as a consequence of being married to Amanda. She is an extrovert. She is also swift to draw comparisons between Mum and me. Apparently, we have many of the same mannerisms. The way I hold my arms and the way I smile are just like her, according to Amanda, who constantly says to me, 'That's your mum.' Sometimes I catch myself in a mirror and I know what she is talking about.

I was born on 30 July 1974 in Calforth Street, in Chapeltown, Leeds – a neighbourhood that gained notoriety some years later as the killing ground of the Yorkshire Ripper. Mum lived on a council estate with Bernard, seven, and George. My brothers were white; I was not.

Mum was a cleaner at a local school and having another child was not going to make life any easier for her. One of Mum's strengths – and she is immensely strong, as well as strong-willed, for someone so tiny, standing barely five feet tall – is her willingness to work hard. No matter how dirty or menial the job, she would do it because she wanted to provide for us. Through her working life she has been mostly a cleaner or caretaker, unafraid of long hours, sometimes juggling two jobs at a time.

I am reliably informed that my mum made a fuss of me from the moment I was born. Perhaps that's what happens to the youngest child in any family, but I know that I can do no wrong in her eyes. There have been times when my behaviour has let her down, but she has never remonstrated with me.

In Chapeltown, there were a lot of Asian and black families. With hindsight, the area was not much better than a ghetto, but for me there was fun and laughter, and the joy of being a child. Not once has my colour been an issue in my family, but I wanted to understand a little of my Caribbean side. My cousin Vinnell is two weeks younger than me and the same colour. Later on, we would go to the Chapeltown carnivals together, following the parade of floats through the streets and sometimes joining in the dancing. I loved the colour and the costumes; the imagination that went into them was amazing. Steel bands accompanied the floats and there would be sound systems blasting music from the houses, all of them playing something different as though it was a competition to find the most funky sound. We tried curried goat, rice and peas, and we ate jerk chicken. There was no other chance to get a taste of my Jamaican heritage. Perhaps I was searching for an identity. All children do that, I suppose, it was just that I didn't have a place to start from.

We moved around from one grim inner-city suburb to another. In Harehills, bordering on Chapeltown, I recall a pub called The Gaiety. It might have been central to the area's entertainment in another age, but by the seventies it was drugs central. It's closed down now, but it was where the local Rastas used to hang out.

In Shadwell, I had my skull cracked open in a stone fight with other kids when I was around six. There really wasn't any malice, just boys being boys. Next stop was Leak Street flats, a high-rise concrete jungle in Hunslet, south Leeds. We lived on the top floor, and the concept was so flawed that the flats were pulled down four years after they were built. The flats had been at the centre of such optimism after slum clearance a few years earlier but were razed to the ground because they were polluted, it was reported, by 'structural defects and massive social problems'.

The salvation in living there was the fact that the flats were practically next door to the Hunslet Boys Club, now called the Hunslet Club for Boys and Girls. This was where I began to play rugby. There was no need to name the code because in Leeds there was only one game of rugby and it was not rugby union. I can still see the space-invaders machines, over on the right of the big hall as you went through the entrance door after paying your 10p subs. I spent a lot of time on those machines.

The club gave us an outlet for the energy kids have to burn. The rugby pitch was across the road, some 250 yards from the hall on the other side of a footbridge. Gypsies had set up camp on some derelict ground near by, and they allowed their dogs to roam free. I was petrified of those dogs – they would often chase us when we came over the footbridge to the rugby pitch. More than once I had to jump on the railway bridge to get away from them. Danny Webb, from Bermondsey in south-east London, who has been leader of the club since 1985, wrote about it in the club's sixtieth anniversary booklet, *Roots and Wings*, in 2000:

It was a delicate situation. Other surrounding areas, derelict following demolition, were a potential breeding ground for delin-quent behaviour. Substance abuse, glue sniffing, was suspected.

Club staff were on alert, liaison with local schools and parents was stepped up. This led to some intensive counselling for a number of young people at risk – not all were members.

Eventually, the gypsies were moved to purpose-planned sites. Danny continued:

The travellers were still in our catchment area so we made tentative contact. An element of trust was established and we organised a fleet of helpers' cars to show them around the club. Something in their culture drew them to our boxing section and before long we had a good number of new recruits for both boxing and rugby.

I went back to visit the club in the autumn of 2002, and Danny told me that between three hundred and four hundred kids use the club each week. He proudly showed me the rows of computers they now have. Some of the youngsters who go there have been excluded from school for one reason or another, so it seems the club's history of providing a safe haven continues unchanged. I don't know what I would have done without it in the evenings and at weekends.

Danny dug out from the archive a picture of me in red strip and Patrick steel toe-capped boots, sat in the middle of the Hunslet Boys Club under-10s. Even then I was the tiniest. Danny told me, 'What made you stand out was your sharpness, your quickness. It was written all over you that you would make a mark in rugby.'

Next door to the Boys Club is the Gospel Hall, where a poster on the wall proclaims 'Jesus said: I am the door. By ME if any man enter in, he shall be saved.' It would be many more years before I came to appreciate and realise the truth of that message; as a schoolboy, religion was a low priority on my agenda. Even so, we often went in to the church because biscuits and drinks were on offer there. They knew how to get an audience, didn't they? We used to spend bonfire night by the chapel, with pie and peas on the menu from the neighbouring pub for all the little rascals from the area.

With Leak Street flats condemned, we moved to the red-brick terraced house in Ingleton Street, Beeston, barely a stone's throw from the Rowland Road Working Men's Club. There used to be a row of old shops across the street, but they had been knocked down. The buildings were never properly cleared so there was a lot of rubble. This shabby-looking area was home to a lot of Asians, as well as mixed-race low-income families.

Close to our house there was a kebab shop and a chippy, now shuttered and barred against vandals, just like the working men's club. Up the street, on the corner of Clovelly Avenue, a small convenience store is still there. The Asian shopkeeper who owned the store at the time used to kill chickens downstairs and, if you chose the wrong moment to go to the shop, he would come up to serve you covered in blood.

Now, in the surrounding streets the shops are all shrouded in steel shutters, indicating that levels of street crime are on the increase. There is a sense of decay and dilapidation far worse than when I lived there. Mum has told me that it is an area where drugs are rife.

We played outside in the street, or more often went to Cross Flats Park, which was a five-minute walk away along roads littered with cheap, clapped-out cars. The park was where everyone met. To get there from our street, we had to pass the Fashion Cloth House on Tempest Road. While it was a clothes shop, the owner had cleverly seen the commercial value of installing a couple of space-invaders machines. That was where my dinner money would disappear – my school, Cross Flats, was situated between the park and the Fashion Cloth House.

The park, huge with a fair number of tall trees, was where we could play whatever sport we fancied, or just fool around on the slide and swings. In summer, we'd use the tennis courts or play crown green bowls on the manicured lawns at the back of the courts. I loved both games. For two years, I was bowls champion and won £3 in prize money. I was getting £1 a week for doing a paper round, so this was a princely sum.

A lot of the Asian lads played cricket and we'd get a game, although there were moments when some of them, having a laugh, I suppose, thought it was better fun to chase us away.

We used the park for all manner of ball games. Occasionally, one of my friends would get hold of an old golf club from some-where. We'd make a hole in the ground and play our version of the British Open. It will be of little surprise to anyone that we hit a few windows in our time.

One of my best friends, Paul, lived a couple of doors down the street from us at No. 54. One day, Paul introduced us to his new dog, Max. Now Max was a cross between a Stafford-shire Bull Terrier and an American Pit Bull. He was white with a black patch on his ear, a dog no one could mistake. Max turned out to have many uses. Sometimes, we'd get out a skate-board and I'd sit on the front with Paul at the back. Max would be on a ten-foot lead and, like a Husky, he would pull us all the way to the park. If Max saw another dog, we knew we were in for a fast ride! When we got to the park with Max, we realised that the days of other boys trying to beat us up were over. No one with any common sense was going to come within a hundred yards of him. At moments when Paul and I weren't seeing eye to eye, he would not hesitate to turn Max on me. I'd have to jump on the climbing frame in the park, and stay there for an hour if necessary. Max was from a bloodline bred for fighting. We saw him have quite a few fights with other dogs and it was scary. He was not prone to letting go once he had something between his teeth.

Our social life centred on the park and sport was central to all we did. We may not have had too many luxuries but we were never short on fun. All we needed was a ball or a racket or a cricket bat.

Despite being a slim, tiny boy, I was in the school football and rugby teams. I cannot say I had any heroes in either game, although I admired Garry Schofield who played rugby league for Leeds. Garry had played at Hunslet Parkside, a club I would later benefit from joining.

Before I was ten years old, I was committed to playing rugby, but one factor that puts children off playing sport in England in winter is the cold climate. Some nights I would be walking through a snowstorm to get to training at the Boys Club. My fingers would be numb with cold, my feet frozen. Little wonder that some kids never turned up on those nights. When people puzzle over why rugby teams in the southern hemisphere have been better than us over the years, one of the reasons has to be that the climate in their countries is more conducive to playing. They live an outdoor life, at the beach or in the parks with a rugby ball or cricket bat. It's easier to get kids to turn out in the sun than in the snow. Looking back, those volunteer coaches who took our sessions had a big job on their hands just to keep everyone involved. When you get home from school and have your tea, the last thing that most kids want to do is go training when it's snowing or hailing. I must have enjoyed it that much that I didn't notice the discomfort. I am glad I stuck at it – and grateful to those who came out to coach us.

Tackling was one of the main attractions of the game for me, never mind that I was small. I loved to get stuck in on the pitch. Rugby sucked all the excess energy from me and sheltered me from taking part in too much mischief. You see kids getting into trouble with drugs or the law through sheer boredom. The friends I had weren't bad lads. Most were like me, very quiet and shy. I suppose we were also naïve. Once, we found a pack of twenty cigarettes and tried to smoke them out of curiosity. The smell and the taste were horrible and cigarettes never interested me again.

As I say, none of us was ever in any kind of real trouble. One day we did discover a telephone box that was not properly secured at the base. We would wait for an opportunity, when there was no one around, and go into the box and extract the money. As children, we never saw any harm in that. If anything, we thought it was the telephone company's fault for not fixing the box, and we enjoyed probably a couple of weeks of income.

One occasion I did think we were in for a roasting was the night we asked someone older than us to get us booze from an off-licence. We were going to a party – I think it was a friend's fourteenth birthday – and we wanted to take alcohol, of course. But as the lad was handing over the drink he had bought for us with our money, the Asian shopkeeper came out and grabbed two of us. He said he was calling the police. He took us in the shop and I don't mind admitting I was scared of what would happen when the police came. Fortunately for us, he had to go out the back to make his call. In a flash, we took the latch off the door and bombed it. We ran and ran through the web of streets, chuffed to have escaped. The threat of the police was one problem – the trouble I'd have been in at home was altogether more worrying. My mum would have been far from amused to have the police return her son.

Somehow, I managed to remain immune to the street crime and the drug culture, which undoubtedly existed. Probably the naughtiest episode of my childhood was when I found a purse with £30 in it when I was playing around with my mate Damien. I'd knocked him off a wall in Rocky Park, a strip of land opposite the Blooming Rose pub, a few streets away from our house. There was a steep bank flanking the park that we used to scream down on our home-made sleds in winter. Damien landed on the purse. We weren't the type to steal, but this didn't feel like stealing. We went straight to a garage shop and bought big bottles of Coke and loads of chocolate. We were absolutely loaded and wondered aloud what we could do with our new-found wealth. We decided to get a bus to visit my cousin Vinnell in Chapeltown. It must have been around 5 November because I know we bought fireworks – and more chocolate. That reflects our innocence, if not necessarily our honesty. The downside to a brilliant day was that we arrived home late for tea. At that age, there had to be a good reason to miss tea, and both our mums were concerned where we were. I think we made up a far from convincing story, got told off and that was it.

This was the extent of the mischief I was involved in as a lad. My mum never allowed me to stay out late. I had to be home and in bed by half past eight. I was the first one in, which

I now accept was a good policy. Some evenings I might try to push my luck, but all that happened was that I would be grounded the next evening. I learned that was an exercise in self-deception.

I didn't hang out much with Bernard or George. They did not need their little brother cramping their style when they were with their own mates. They did get asked how they could have a brother who was a different colour from them, and I'm sure there were times when this was not easy for them. Kids can be wicked and cruel when they want to be. But to Bernard and George, I was never less than an equal. I think they have always been proud of me. Their father would come to see them sometimes. He was always nice to me. He sent me birthday cards; I was happy to share him with Bernard and George, even if we didn't see that much of him.

As characters, Bernard and George are not in the least alike. Bernard is quiet, George much more laddish. Bernard loved motorbikes, more so than George although he rode one, too. They had a scrambler and what we called a 'plackey', which was a Honda 50cc without an exhaust. It made a horrible noise when it was started. I was riding on the back of these bikes before I was fourteen. We would go through the woods, sometimes getting chased by park patrolmen, who had big powerful BMW machines, but we never seemed to get caught. As a teenager, George was into snazzy clothes. Neither of my brothers was the least bit sporty. Mum can remember that one of her younger brothers played rugby in Scotland; otherwise there is no known family link to suggest why I should play to the standard I do.

I went just once to watch my brothers play football. It was

a cold, wintry day and I suppose they must have been forced to be part of the team. George locked himself in the car with the heater on and refused to come out because of the weather. Bernard scored the winning goal when the ball stuck in the mud and he kicked it into the goal from three yards. That was the only time I saw them anywhere near a sports field.

When they'd had too much to drink, their brotherly rivalry could easily spill over into violent confrontation, but they looked out for one another in school and on the streets. I remember them telling me stories of their school going to fight another school in a pre-arranged bust-up. They'd have big fights. That happened to me once, at Cross Flats middle school. Some other school came to meet us on the park. Their boys were lined up about fifty yards from us and when someone yelled 'Charge', we ran towards them and they ran towards us. My friends and I chickened out and put the handbrakes on. It ended with the so-called hardest boy in their school brawling with the toughest kid from Cross Flats. Everyone else stood around and shouted, 'Fight, fight, fight.'

School life was hard. There were a lot of people around with whom, if you had the choice, you would not really want to share a room. There were boys I was scared of – real hard nuts. I made sure I didn't tread on their toes, but you couldn't be seen to be too soft or they could make life miserable. I seemed to get the balance more or less right.

Mum had battled on alone, working all hours as a cleaner and then a school caretaker, until she met Richard Robinson when I was not much older than eight. He worked in a whole-sale fruit and vegetable market in Leeds, tidying up. I was really happy for her when they married a few years later at a local

19

registry office. I was in middle school and had to change my name, although my brothers did not. It was right that I should have the same name as my mum, now Mrs Robinson. Yet for a boy around twelve years old, there was a bit of stigma. I was asked if I'd been adopted. It was also strange when the register in class was called because I'd forget I was no longer Jason Brannan, but Jason Robinson. I'd sometimes put the wrong name at the top of my written work, too.

While I had grown accustomed to going to work with Mum after finishing school or in the holidays – I enjoyed helping her polish the floors with a big industrial cleaner that you needed a licence to operate, or so it seemed – I now had another source of income. I'd go with Richard to the market. I was used to earning my own money from an early age – a work ethic I am proud to have inherited from Mum.

Richard would bring home produce from the market, some written off, some more dubiously acquired I suspect. I would make up parcels of the fruit and vegetables and we would go out selling them from a trailer Richard attached to the back of his car. We would drive to Bell Isle, a couple of miles away, and park outside a working men's club. I suppose, looking back, it sounds Del Boy-ish, but the money was useful and needed. I didn't mind packing the parcels, but I was not keen about selling them from the trailer. Call it teenage embarrassment. After all, it hardly enhances your street-cred.

These were times when making some extra money was important, no matter how bizarre the circumstances may seem now. It was a fact of life that as soon as a house was boarded up the slates would be gone in no time. Lead had a price, too. When the Leak Street flats were coming down, people were taking any stuff they could lay their hands on. When the buildings opposite the flats were demolished, we would take sandwiches with us because there was so much to collect for re-sale. A favourite game was jumping on to mattresses from first-floor windows of the disused buildings.

Other times, I remember burning wire to strip it down to lead to take to the scrapyard. When it had been weighed, you'd get the going rate. It seemed normal – you needed to be enterprising to survive. At the market, I would drive the little electric wagons about; then, when I was older, I was paid to mend pallets. I'd be there with a hammer and nails and repair a big heap of them that had been broken in the market.

In the early years, I did consider Richard to be the father I never had. He showed an interest in rugby and came to watch me play. There were plenty of good times with him in our little house before the violence erupted. He used to make home brew and there was a barrel at the top of the stairs leading to the cellar. Down there, we had a darts board and we might all play once in a while. I would be delegated to get beers for Mum and Richard from the barrel, and I would be allowed a shandy. I can't say I liked it – it was pretty strong stuff.

Holidays were the best. We would rent a caravan in Bridlington or Scarborough. Then Richard decided we should have our own van. Over the years, he had all kinds of vehicles – 90 per cent of them came from Mally's second-hand yard by Rocky Park. None of them cost much more than £100 – a 'long 'un' as he used to say. There was a VW camper van with a concertina roof that I remember got us as far as six miles from home once and never went any further. Another time, the clips holding down the roof broke. As we drove along the motorway, my mum was in the back of the van swinging off the roof to keep it closed. Smoke was coming off her hands. We had a Dodge van, which had once done sterling service for BT. It was green and we nicknamed it the Green Goddess.

Another memorable experience was trying to navigate a steeply rising hill in a red Ford Escort van Richard had bought. The hill was probably not much more than quarter of a mile long. Richard was dropping down through the gears as soon as the road started to rise, and we were going slower and slower. I was sat in the back and by the time Richard had engaged first gear, there was a queue of hundreds of cars behind us.

Some other cars we had didn't even make it up the hills. Our Vauxhall Viva was metallic, very sporty looking with big wide wheels, but the weight in the car used to rub on the wheels and bring us to a halt. We would pull over and empty stuff out of the car to reduce the weight to get up the hill. Then we'd get out and Richard would have to go back to collect our things. But if the journeys were a little unpredictable, the holidays themselves were great. Staying in a caravan park was never less than a big adventure.

I was sixteen years old when I went abroad for the first time. Damien came with Richard, Mum and me to Kavos in Greece. Damien and I hired motorbikes. I had gears on mine, while his just seemed to rev and go. Unluckily for us – or rather for Damien – we were travelling at roughly 30 miles per hour when a donkey strayed into the road in front of us. I managed to miss it and stay upright, but Damien came off his bike and skidded down the road for what seemed like forever. He left most of the skin from the back of his legs on the tarmac and scratched his bike rather noticeably. We realised our alibi for the damage was not altogether convincing. Who was going to believe that a stray donkey had caused the accident?

We plucked up the courage to return the bikes, forlornly hoping that the owner of the hire company would not spot the damage to Damien's bike. When he saw what state it was in, we spluttered that our insurance would cover the cost of the repair. That plan had one flaw – we had no insurance cover. The owner – and he was a big guy – said, 'You pay me . . . or the doctor.' He was an intimidating figure and we didn't have any money. We were near to tears when we went to fetch Richard and Mum. They had a go at the owner, but he was not a man to be easily dissuaded. We ended up paying him some money for the damage. I think we escaped lightly. At least we lived to tell the tale.

In all, I think Richard Robinson was in my life for around nine years. I had respect for him for some of the things he did for us, but that went when the violence started and I watched what Mum was put through.

Mum still sees him about town. Amazingly, she has no anger left.

3

MAKING THE GRADE

'The difference between a successful person and the others is not a lack of knowledge but a lack of will.'

VINCE LOMBARDI

As I entered my teenage years, I went from Hunslet Boys Club to play for Hunslet Parkside. Some friends had joined the club and I knew it was going to offer a better grade of rugby. Parkside was renowned as a breeding ground, giving those who had talent and worked hard to polish it a chance to gain entry to the professional ranks. When I joined as a thirteen year old, Garry Schofield's mum Jean was tealady. Her son had begun his career at the club, so we knew what was possible. Garry was a fantastic player for Leeds and Great Britain. Jean was still making the teas at Parkside in the winter of 2002.

But when I joined Parkside, secretary Colin Cooper did not suppose for a moment he was looking at a lad headed for the professional game. I was a knobbly-kneed scrum-half and still a little mouse. Colin's wife Una remembers the first time she set eyes on me. 'You were a little lad huddled in the corner of our dressing room with your bag on your knee,' she told me. 'You sat there for a long time before saying a word.' That was me.

24

The Coopers have been the heartbeat of Hunslet Parkside since Colin began with the club in 1973. By his estimation, over two hundred boys have become professionals after learning the game there. The club runs teams for under eights and upwards. Colin's unselfish work these past thirty years – together with the efforts of those he recruited to assist at the club – allowed boys like me to dream. With Una, he seemed to organise all that went on. They had a scruffy little dog, Prince, that was everywhere you turned. They treated Prince like a son.

We trained a couple of nights a week and while we lived in Beeston I used to get to the club on the number 86 bus. Later, Mum found a job as a caretaker at a school not far from Hunslet Parkside's ground. This post included housing and we moved to Tremont Gardens. The area, far from being affluent, was nevertheless an improvement on Beeston. All I wanted to do by now was play rugby, so it never bothered me where we lived as long as Mum was there.

Steve Kempton and Steve Hamill were the coaches, and they made training fun as well as instructive. Their wives, Avis and Carol, did the laundry. Steve Hamill was a bus driver, a real character who used to wind up people. He was forever joking, but he'd tell it how it was. He loved boys to get stuck in on the pitch. His heart was in the club; he just wanted us to do well. Steve Kempton spent hours with us, teaching us how to think as well as play. He became a scout for Wigan, I believe.

We did not have our own transport at the club and Colin used to borrow an old banger from a local church to get us to the games. It had curtains on the windows. Later, he gained access to a community bus; only trouble was it belonged to a community on the other side of Leeds so he had to trek across the city to get it. Parents rallied round with cars.

Each year, we would have a club outing to Blackpool or Bridlington for the day. If we were going to Blackpool, we would play a game on the way at somewhere like Widnes; if it was Bridlington, there would be a hard game in Hull.

On the pitch, I suppose my strength was beating people. From that early age, I had a good sidestep and speed off the mark. They are blessings I have reason to be grateful for to this day. I was always a runner. I like to think it wasn't a matter of being selfish, more a question of playing to my strengths. That is the first requirement any coach seeks from his players after all.

Apparently, I took time to assert myself. According to Colin, until I was fifteen, I was just another lad coming for a game of rugby, small-framed and with no obvious talent. It had been easy to see that Garry Schofield and Dave Creasser would make it as professionals, but I was just one of the lads who played the game and had his cup of soup or tea. Colin says, 'We had a lot of those lads and we have a lot of them still. Basically, I think I've got more one-parent families than the benefit office. I've always recognised that rugby is keeping most of my kids out of trouble.' That was the case with me, as Colin well knows. He used to come and fetch me from Ingleton Street, so he knew where I came from. At Parkside, it became clear that rugby was my outlet in life. If I hadn't taken to rugby, I could have gone another way, and at fifteen I began to show real potential. Colin referred to me as a matchbreaker, by which he meant I was very fast and could produce a flash of inspiration to break a game. It was not something that could be coached.

We had a good spirit at the club, a team full of character. One lad, Recky, was way ahead of the rest of us in build. We were still kids; he was a young man. He had facial hair, big legs and was as hard as nails. That team grew close, we certainly played as one. If somebody was in need of help, everyone pitched in.

As well as laughter, we experienced sadness in the cruellest manner, just at the moment we were supposed to be celebrating being young and indestructible. Wayne Kelly was one of those lads who sucked the juice from life. He was always game for a laugh and he could handle himself on the pitch. He was immensely popular and Colin always said he was the spitting double for Vinnie Jones, whose footballing travels brought him to Leeds for a spell before he found himself an unlikely Hollywood star.

When Wayne fell down at the Christmas party in 1990, there was no sense of alarm. We were all so young, all so optimistic, fantasising about going out from Hunslet to conquer the world. I just thought he'd had one too many beers. Someone said later he had gone to the toilet and collapsed. Someone else said his heart had stopped. An ambulance was called, of course. We were all stunned by the tragedy unfolding before us. One moment we had been laughing with him, like always; the next he was being driven away in an ambulance. The party came to an abrupt end; everyone was in a daze, sad and confused, weeping and afraid.

Wayne died on the way to hospital. I had never been to a funeral before, and there was so much grief in so many young people with so much to be optimistic about. But the one thing I will never forget is seeing his dad crying. I can picture it like it was yesterday.

Colin ensured a plaque was hung in the club pavilion in memory of Wayne. Sadly, another plaque was added in 2002 after another Parkside boy, Kyle Adams, was killed in a road accident. Carl Pratt – one of the lads who made it from Hunslet to the Great Britain team – donated the cap he won against Australia in 2002 and it was buried with young Kyle.

The classroom was never a place where I shone. With over thirty kids in the class at Matthew Murray High School, it was easy to get left behind. I was too shy to put my hand up to ask a teacher to explain what I had not understood. Can you imagine how the others would have taken the mickey? I could, and I was not going to give them the satisfaction. Still, I know I could have done much better at school.

I studied for exams in English, maths, biology and history, and I took a construction course, involving bricklaying, plumbing and joinery, one day a week at a neighbouring college. I don't think I did any revision. I really don't know what planet I was on. Only when I had a rugby ball in my hands did I have a sense of self-worth. I knew that I possessed some talent and on the rugby pitch I was assured and confident. I was in control. I could make an impact. I could do all the things I couldn't do in the classroom because of my reticence and natural shyness.

After a time, I was selected to play for Leeds & District. From there, I was chosen for Yorkshire. I went for a trial for the England Under-18 team but I was not chosen. A lad called Gareth Stevens was selected. His dad was something in the game, I think. I was embittered at the time but, being honest, he was a better ball-handler than I was. I was just a runner. Even so, I still nurtured an ambition to become a professional.

I was a ball-boy at Leeds and, while I had no idea what the

pressure must have been like on the players, I can recount that just retrieving the ball when it went out of play induced a bout of nervousness that I had not known before.

Eventually, Leeds invited me to go to see them. The coach, David Ward, wanted me to sign, and that was clearly a more exciting prospect than signing for Hunslet, an altogether smaller club. Leeds took me on a summer camp and asked me to play for the A team at York, but the game clashed with Parkside's annual fixture with Wigan St Pats – one year we would play in Wigan, the next they'd come to us, and it was our turn to host them. David Ward gave me an ultimatum – play for Leeds or miss out. Wigan St Pats was our top game of the year and I couldn't let Parkside down. David Ward found it hard to understand that I put the club before Leeds. It broke my heart when they told me I wouldn't make the grade. To be told that at sixteen, just when I thought there was a career awaiting me, was very hard to take. Professional sport is not an arena where sentiment is paid more than lip service. Later, Colin told me that he was convinced that if Leeds had taken me on, I would have been wasted. 'I've seen so many lads taken there and wasted,' he said.

But I was fortunate. Unbeknown to me, Eric Hawley had his eye on me. He was the man who had discovered Ellery Hanley, one of the giants of the modern game who played an immense role in Wigan's wonderfully successful era from the mid eighties. Eric had been watching me since I was fourteen and playing for Parkside. You can't sign professionally until you are sixteen. Here's how he tells it:

Now Jason was a ball-boy with Leeds at Headingley and there is a tendency for lads to want to sign for their local club. For Jason that was always going to be Leeds rather than Hunslet, who, with respect, were not in the same class. Jason had been training at Headingley and I had heard they were going to offer him terms. I thought that was that. But then I heard a whisper on the grapevine that they weren't signing Jason, but another scrum-half called Gareth Stevens. I had not long since joined Wigan and I thought here's my chance. The season was just starting with Hunslet Parkside. I looked at my fixture list and saw they were playing at Featherstone Sports Centre, so I went along. There is quite a long walk from the changing rooms to the pitch, and I walked alongside Jason and the team coach Steve Kempton. I told them that I had heard what had happened with Leeds and that now I was with Wigan, I was going to watch Jason for the next three or four weeks. To be honest, I could see that Jason was still disappointed with what went on at Leeds; the kid was really down. I watched him again the following week and he was playing just as I knew he could. Jason had what scouts look for – elusive pace. Sounds silly, but for a scrum-half he wasn't that quick around the base of the scrum. He used to go on diagonal runs and bring the opposition across. As soon as he spotted a gap, whoosh, he was away. And he was born with that little jink, that sidestep of his. Usually I watch a lad over four to six weeks, leave them alone, then go back. But with Jason, I knew I dare not wait. Two games were enough for me.

On the next Wednesday night, Wigan were playing at Wakefield and I drove over. The Wigan team coach was in the car park and the directors were still sat on board. At away matches, they'd sit on the coach until thirty or forty minutes before kick-off, and then they would go to the boardroom They had a coffee machine on the coach and they liked to have a cup before going into the ground. Maurice Lindsay was the chairman and when I climbed on board, he said, 'Ah, just the man I want to have a word with. I've heard there's an exceptional lad playing in the Hunslet area.'

'Oh, aye,' I replied, 'is it Jason Robinson?'

'Yes. How do you know?' asked Lindsay.

'I've been watching him for the past two weeks. I want to sign him. I've come to speak to you about bringing him over to next week's board meeting.'

'Great, go ahead,' said Lindsay.

I contacted Jason who was delighted. I also contacted Steve. In all my career – and I was in my thirty-third year as a scout in December 2002 having been with Bradford Northern, Leeds (twice), Wigan and Bradford Bulls – I had never had a coach with me because a lad's terms are personal. But Jason had no father he could take, and, as lovely as his mother Dorothy is, she felt this was not something she knew anything about. Jason asked for Steve to come. In the car on the way over to Wigan, Jason was quiet as usual. He was always quiet, a gentleman in comparison to some of the kids I have come across. I introduced him to the board and Jason signed that night, getting a £15,000 signing-on fee. As he was going to play for the Academy, his wages weren't that special. It was like an apprenticeship. He was probably on a £20 win bonus.

At an early game, Wigan's coach John Monie was watching Jason when he pulled me over.

'Can Jason pass a ball?' he asked me. I understood what he meant. Jason was doing what he always did – running diagonally, waiting for the gap, then jinking through it and away. Nobody could keep up with him, so he didn't have to pass.

Of course I agreed to join Wigan without further debate – as if I was ever going to decline any kind of contract. Here I was, just out of school, being asked to sign for Wigan, the Manchester United of rugby league. To what part of that was I going to say no?

I came out of school without any formal qualifications and,

if I'm honest, I assumed I was going to be a bricklayer. I was set up for a job by Jack Lunn, whose company sponsored Hunslet Parkside. At the interview I will always remember that a condition of my employment was to ease back on my rugby commitments. This cut to the core of what I wanted from life so I rejected the offer. Instead, I followed a lead that my mum had found. She had seen an advertisement for a job at a company called Ultrasonic Cleaning Services, and the attraction was that their premises were on a little industrial estate not far from home. Company boss Bob Marshall seemed like a decent man and I was hired at around £50 a week. We used to strip paint, clean castings and recycle metal in acid and caustic tanks. If it wanted cleaning, UCS could do it.

While working at UCS, I was training with Wigan, some sixty miles away. I was content for a time. We played crib in Bob's office at lunchtimes for a penny a point. His brother would often pop in for a game. On the shopfloor, I had to wear rubber boots, a floor-length apron and gloves because we came into contact with acid. It seemed in no time at all I was on wages of £125 a week. I could not spend all that.

But the demands of Wigan began to encroach on the job. In order to train, I had to start at 8 a.m. and finish at 4 p.m. It soon became evident that this was too much. Wigan wanted me to go full-time, to concentrate on my development in the game. They readily agreed to make up the wages I would be losing and at seventeen, I was going to be paid more money than I knew what to do with to play a game I would have played for nothing. It was obvious to me there was little else to do other than resign from UCS.

I thought that's how events unfolded, until I returned to see

Bob Marshall in late autumn 2002. Bob had not changed; he was still gregarious, still smiling and still cleaning anything from reconditioned engines to pipework. But Bob insisted I had not resigned. He told me, 'At the golf club, they say it's my claim to fame that I am the man who sacked Jason Robinson! You wanted to take a week's holiday in a busy week and I couldn't let you off. It was a shame; you were a good worker. I do remember that you started early and took a shower before you left – and sometimes, those crib games meant lunchtime went on a bit.'

Returning to UCS, the strongest memory, apart from Bob's sense of humour, was the smell. It hung in the air, and could stick to you like an unwanted scent. You also had to be so careful with what was in the acid baths. But I was lucky. In the one proper job I have had, I worked with decent, down-to-earth people.

I bought a Ford Escort Eclipse with my signing-on fee, a much classier car than my first set of wheels. I had a half share in a brown Maxi, a model with a dented wing and a 1750cc engine with a gearbox that you needed to double de-clutch. My share cost £35. Of course, the car couldn't be used on public roads; it had no chance of ever passing the MoT. My new(ish) Escort was also rather different from the cars Richard used to drive us around in, that series of £100 specials bought from Mally's.

In 2002, Colin Cooper introduced a Hall of Fame at Hunslet Parkside, and I am honoured to say that I was inducted with Dave Heron, Dave Creasser, Garry Schofield, Sonny Nichol, James Lowes and Carl Pratt. Each of us has a shirt hung on the wall and Colin is especially proud of one particular photograph of Garry, Sonny and me playing in the same Great Britain team. 'You three represent a ten-year period of history at the club,' he says. 'How many other amateur clubs can boast such riches?'

I gave Colin a wristwatch after signing for Wigan. Apparently, he's still got it in the box it came in. Later, he told me I was the only one to give him and the two Steves thank-you presents.

4

WALKING IN A
WEMBLEY
WONDERLAND

'Some people set high standards for themselves, they come out early and stay late . . . funny how they are usually the winners.'

VINCE LOMBARDI

I ceased to be an amateur the day after my seventeenth birthday. My dream had come true beyond my wildest expectation – not only was I a professional rugby player, but I was at the biggest club in Britain. But all dreams are interrupted when you are returned to the reality of the moment. For me, it was awakening to the fact that there is a quantum leap between signing for a club like Wigan and actually breaking into the first team. You look around and wonder if you will ever be qualified to play at the required level.

It was a daunting prospect. I felt dwarfed by all those around me, in reputation as well as size. I was alone in an alien world. Although it was barely sixty miles from Wigan to Leeds, I might as well have been in another galaxy. I had no support system, no Mum to cook for me, do my laundry or talk with. If that sounds soft, it is simply a reflection of how it was. I must have incurred a large phone bill just calling Mum, wanting to know that she was fine, but also needing some reassurances. With my natural shyness, the only chance I had to make friends at the club was to show what I could do on the pitch. I knew the only way to gain respect was to illustrate the contribution I had to make. That is only achieved with time.

But then the club's Australian coach, John Monie, decided for reasons only he knows to invite me to stay with him and his family in their home outside town. I think the idea was that I'd stay for a few weeks, but I ended up living with John, his wife Julie and son Stephen for closer to nine months. They treated me like a son. As well as having home comforts – in truth, comforts far beyond those I'd known growing up in those harsh suburbs of Leeds – I was also getting a fast-track education in the game. John is a coach of outstanding ability. He came from the Australian game and made Wigan the greatest rugby league club this country has known, before or since. We watched videos at home and talked things through. His briefings were priceless. I cannot imagine how green I was, how naïve, how devoid of knowledge. John worked diligently to rectify those shortcomings.

Stephen had a few games for the Academy team. Then he got a job at the Riverside Club, right by the rugby club. John says I was a little wild and I do recall one embarrassing episode after I'd been out drinking. It was about four o'clock in the morning and snowing, and I suppose I thought I'd go to sleep in the car. My foot must have lodged on the accelerator, so there I was in this quiet little village fast asleep with the car revving full blast. A neighbour knocked on the front door, and they got me indoors and up to bed.

John had been a coach for twenty years and coped with a lot of young players feeling their way, discovering what goes on in life. I had plenty of self-discipline in the game, but I was certainly no saint.

To start with at Wigan, I was played as a half-back. In the junior divisions, the coaches tended to put me close to the ball because of my speed, but I wasn't really a half-back. With my explosive pace, I was more suited to wing play. I didn't have the endurance a half-back needs. My great attribute was that I was so quick off the mark, but I did need a little time to recover. John described Wigan as a jigsaw puzzle – I was a little piece over on one side of it. He says:

Wigan got so far ahead of everybody that people became jealous. To bring a young guy into first grade and place him in a key position is too hard. Jason wasn't very old and I felt I had to protect him. That meant getting him away from the action, getting him out where he could have a look at what went on in the middle of the park. His contribution would be what I knew he could do.

If you throw a kid right into the middle of the park where the action is, it's pretty easy for some big forward who's on the wrong side of thirty and done a lot of tough yards and a lot of tough years to get hold of him and target him. If the confidence goes in those early days, some kids never get it back. We were very careful with Jason. He couldn't be spotted too much on the wing because we had such a good side; the opposition weren't really going to target him. That was the team's greatness, actually. We had so many players who could beat an opponent one on one. It was just a lethal attack with Dean Bell, Shaun Edwards and Andy Gregory. The last two were the champion half-back pairing in the game in England.

From the beginning, Jason never had any fear of confrontation or any fear of doing hard work, which really is a bit of a formula for great players. Great players are usually great trainers, they work harder than most people away from the game. His preparation was always really good – he had great role models in the team. He didn't mind having a collision if that's the way it had to be. Jason didn't play with any fear factor. The great players can make the bench stand up, even make their coaches stand up. When they get the ball in their hands and you can see who's in front of them, you think, 'Gee, that's not enough to stop him.' They bring you from your seat. It's fantastic. I had no doubts Jason would become one of the great players.

Only when you retrace the years do you fully appreciate what some people have done for you. It was a blessing to have John and Julie Monie there at a critical period in my life – and not just to put me to bed the night I fell asleep with my foot jammed hard against the accelerator in the car parked in their drive. Believe me, there were to be far more embarrassing moments than that in the years I drank with the thirst of a sailor on shore leave.

As coach, John was the man who gave me my opportunity. He had seen me play at half-back in the Academy team – the reserves – and watched me in the sevens tournament prior to the 1992 season, and then he picked me on the wing. I would have played anywhere, but the wing is where I stayed for the remainder of my career in rugby league.

How fast am I? I could not tell you. I have never run a hundred metres against the clock. There never seemed any point. Running in perfect conditions in spikes on an athletics track is rather different from running with studs on wet grass with four lads trying to stop you. The speed I possess is quickness off the mark. It has always been my greatest asset. It is why I back myself to beat the first defender.

Even now, in training, I marvel at players who have good hands. I'd love to pass like them. Yet when we are playing touch rugby, they tell me they marvel at the way I dance all over the place, not allowing anyone to catch me, and beating people in tight spaces.

From the beginning, playing for Wigan was a massive thing. I may not have studied hard for my history exams but I knew that I had joined a club with a great tradition. So many outstanding players had played for them. I was at a club where there were so many current internationals that I knew I would have to be at my sharpest to seize any opportunity arising. Clearly, I did enough to impress John Monie. Having not played that many games for the Academy side, I was selected for my first-team debut against Hull on 29 August 1992. Two things were apparent from the moment I made it into the team – you could take nothing for granted, and, as a Wigan player, you were not allowed to be average.

There were a lot of dedicated players at the club – Shaun Edwards, Joe Lydon, Kelvin Skerrett, Martin Dermott, Andy Platt, Denis Betts, Billy McGinty, Phil Clarke and newly signed Martin Offiah, all of whom had spent that summer playing for Great Britain in a Test series in Australia. With other players including New Zealanders Dean Bell and Frano Botica, a convert from rugby union, along with Sam Panapa and teenaged prodigy Andy Farrell, younger even than me, the squad was an enviable one. The rivalry for places was intense, but, in my experience, never cut-throat – it was simply a lot of people working hard because they wanted to play.

Wigan was the first club to have an entirely professional playing staff, I believe. That professionalism manifested itself in the players' attitude to training, as well as playing. In weight training there was always a competition to see who could lift the heaviest weight. It's one of those incomprehensible traits that surfaces whenever men are together. Whether you perform on the international stage or in the local park, put a bunch of guys together and we will compete by instinct.

With such competition, the pressure of expectation once you are in the team is enormous – over 20,000 spectators watching you, following your every move, assessing whether you are good enough for their team. Some players freeze at first; others excel in the environment. I found the atmosphere exciting rather than intimidating, and I was concentrating on learning my new position as a winger – although just because John wanted me to be on the right wing, I never felt that justified straying too far from the action. I used to do a lot of hard yards from out of the 20 metre area. I would go in at dummy half and run from there – I suppose it was a style that had not been seen too much from a winger before. In those days, a winger tended to remain out wide.

It was tough sometimes, putting your body on the line waiting to get smashed, but it was the way I wanted to play, not a coaching directive. I have always liked to be central to the game; I was getting some good yards and the forwards were happy about that. I was looking for approval, a sense of belonging. Taking the odd crunching tackle seemed a reasonable price to pay for acceptance. On that score, club captain Dean Bell was of great assistance in my early days at Central Park. I learned a lot from him, especially the importance of mental toughness. He was the type of guy who never took a backward step. He led from the front – and with him looking out for me, nobody took advantage.

Then there was Shaun Edwards. The little man is an institution at Wigan. Has anyone been more decorated in the game?
Basically, he's done everything. He read the game like few men
can. He drew opponents, then nonchalantly slipped a team-
mate through a hole in their defence. It is a skill only those
with real vision on the pitch can master. He was feisty and his
temper burned on a short fuse, but that was his way of dealing
with those who might try to bully or intimidate him. Anyone
who played against Shaun will testify that trying to get him to
back down was a waste of time. Shaun was never going to be
anywhere other than in your face. His support play was also
extraordinary; he just popped up everywhere. Against Swinton
in the Lancashire Cup in 1992, he scored ten tries.

Five months earlier, Offiah had also run in ten tries for Wigan,
against Leeds in the Premiership Trophy. It cost Wigan
£440,000 to sign him from neighbouring rivals Widnes, and
the investment proved to be a shrewd one. Martin is the best
rugby league winger I have ever seen. He was a one-off, no
question. He would be the first to admit that he never liked
being at the core of the game, in those places where you could
get roughed up. But when it came to scoring tries, there was
no one like Martin. His speed took my breath away, never mind
his. It was worth the entrance money just to see Martin in full
flight. If your life depended on a try being scored, you'd want
Martin to have the ball in his hands with daylight on the wing.
With players of his calibre, it was small wonder that Wigan were
the team all others feared.

Imagine the thrill of scoring a try on my debut that August
afternoon against Hull. I took an inside ball from Shaun
Edwards, beat one defender and scrambled over the line.

Absolutely amazing! From that moment, I became a regular first-team player.

My first season had a tumultuous climax at Wembley, where we met Widnes in the Challenge Cup final. The old stadium with the fabled twin towers may have been condemned to meet the bulldozers, like the Leak Street flats that I once called home, but to a rugby league fan there was never a more eagerly awaited day than a match at Wembley. If your team was involved, it was more than a game; it was a pilgrimage. People joined savings clubs to ensure they had the money safely stowed for the big occasion. For one gloriously mad day, London was subjected to an invasion force from the north of England. At first light, fleets of coaches and mini buses would be loaded with crates of beer. The motorways south became a seething mass of cars and buses decorated with scarves flying from the windows as thousands of men, women and children headed for a land that, for most of them, for 364 days of the year was as foreign, cold and unattractive to them as the snowfields of Alaska. But on Challenge Cup final day, there was nowhere else they would rather have been than London. I made sure my mum was at the game.

Like any boy who played the game, I fantasised about one day playing in a Cup final. But as I was running across the footbridge past the gypsies and their angry dogs to play on that worn pitch in the red jersey of Hunslet Boys Club, you would have found no one prepared to wager a pound that seven years later I'd be on the Wigan team bus headed for Wembley. Two days before the final, thousands turned up to wave us off from Central Park and that's when you understand the importance of the game to the fans. The excitement within just builds and builds until finally you are driving from the team hotel to the stadium. On the bus, you feel the adrenaline pumping as a motivational video with booming soundtrack is shown. At the stadium, there are thousands of supporters congregated near the big gates, which the bus driver has to negotiate to deliver you to the inner sanctum. From the coach, you walk straight into the changing room. One impression from that first time remains to this day – inside was the biggest bath I have ever seen.

I have never been superstitious. I have always thought it a lot of nonsense when someone says something like, 'I always put my right boot on first because it brings me luck.' Who are they trying to kid? So, the day they forget and put their boots on in the wrong order they have a ready-made excuse for when something goes wrong. It's amazing how much that can affect people. To me, it's a sign of mental weakness. You have got your excuse in first.

Much of what took place in that first Wembley final is a blur. Stood in the tunnel waiting to go out, I do remember there was noise like I had never heard before – rolling noise that hit you as you strode across the perimeter on to the pitch, noise that would not be silenced. Brilliant, just brilliant. I tried to focus, looking ahead and not making eye contact with any of the opposition players lined up beside us. I knew they were there, but I had to think of my own job.

Wigan fans had become accustomed to being an integral part of the occasion. The club had monopolised the Challenge Cup, winning it for the previous five years. Unsurprisingly, on 1 May 1993, Widnes were rank outsiders.

Twice Widnes led, with tries from Richie Eyres and Kurt

Sorensen, both converted by Jonathan Davies, once an icon of the Welsh rugby union team, but each time we came back, through tries by Kelvin Skerrett and Dean Bell. With his second conversion, Frano Botica, a lethal kicker, broke the Wigan record of 176 goals in a season, which had been held by Fred Griffiths since 1959. I cannot pretend to be either a statistician or an historian, so happily confess to the fact that I am indebted for this information to Les Hoole's book, *The Rugby League Challenge Cup*. We won the game 24–14, due to a try from Sam Panapa and two more goals from Botica. Widnes finished a man down after Eyres was sent off in the sixty-fifth minute when he was adjudged to have elbowed Offiah in the head. I also recall that near the end Bobby Goulding caught me round the head with a late tackle and there was a brief, but ugly, brawl.

None of this registers, though, as much as the feeling of elation, bewilderment and sheer shock, walking round Wembley holding the Cup. At that moment, I wondered if it could ever get any better. I don't remember much of the night that followed.

5

ON WIGAN BEER

Surprise, surprise, I woke up with a hangover, but I knew the
cure – all I needed was a drink.

The bus ride from London back to Wigan was like a works
outing, only better. As sportsmen, if you can't celebrate after
winning a cup, when can you celebrate? We played hard and
we partied hard. By the time we reached the town, most of us
were nicely topped up from the night before.

As usual, there was an open-topped bus booked to carry us
on a triumphal tour of Wigan. The fans never tired of this ritual
and thousands lined the roads to cheer us on our return from
London. At Central Park, the pitch was a sea of people dressed
in cherry and white, ready to hail the conquering heroes home.
Over the public address system, Tina Turner was blasting out
'Simply the Best'; it was our unofficial anthem by now. As usual,
Denis Betts, a hard-working forward, offered himself as a night-
club act, giving the fans his unique rendition of the song 'I Feel
Good'. They loved him for his enthusiasm, I think. Everyone

was on a high, not only from winning but also from the amount of alcohol that had been taken.

Another tradition had to be observed. I had been reliably informed that the trashing of our dressing room was now custom and practice on our return from the Challenge Cup final. While the fans were singing and chanting outside, the players were inside smashing up the place we called home during the season. The showers were ripped out and nothing escaped the carnage. The dressing room soon looked like a demolition squad had strayed into the place with a contract to rearrange the furniture and fittings by nightfall. No one from the club said a word in protest. I don't suppose that ever happened after Manchester United or Arsenal won the Cup, but some traditions are stranger to comprehend than others. As we took the dressing room apart, we carried on drinking.

I had been exposed to the dangers of alcohol from an early age but I did not heed the warning signs. I was now heavily into a drinking culture of my own at Wigan. I drank to overcome my diffident personality. After a drink or two, I felt more at ease and lost some of my natural shyness. Where I was previously reluctant to talk, I became more inclined to speak after a few beers. I also needed to fit in, or so I thought at the time.

I had by now moved into a terraced house that the club had bought me, close enough to Central Park for visiting supporters to park right outside my front-room window. Arthur Thomas, a club director, owned a decorating company and he kindly arranged for the downstairs rooms to be redecorated. I had no idea about that stuff.

I'd get an empty feeling when I was alone in the house, and I hated it. I used to wait for the phone to ring and for someone to ask, 'Are you coming out?' Everybody who called knew the answer before they rang. If one of the players was going out to Wakefield on Monday, I'd be there. If another suggested Oldham on Tuesday, I'd be with him; it might be Liverpool on Wednesday and Wigan on Thursday. Where we went was of no real importance. Being part of the scene was what mattered. We were not out for a social drink, either. The ethos was rather more basic. Our pattern conformed to a single ambition – to see how many drinks we could get down in as little time as possible. It's silly, I know, but that's how we behaved. Everybody I knew used to go to the pubs or clubs and get drunk. I just got into the same habit. It's how I lived. When I went out, I drank with a furious haste. With each beer, I'd take vodka or some other kind of chaser. We didn't have a few pints, we had barrels. On some nights, we could easily each drown a bottle of vodka as well.

I was impressionable and easily indoctrinated into the ways of some of the team. I was also adopted by the front row – Kelvin Skerrett, Neil Cowie and Martin Hall, great lads on the pitch and something of a legend in the pub. We used to joke about Martin not having a throat. He just poured pints down, never appearing to swallow.

When you're out with the lads, I suppose your macho side demands to be heard. You want to be accepted and that means you are not prepared to go against the grain. Perhaps this is peer pressure, but I needed little excuse to be involved. Our drinking could begin as soon as training ended. The nearest pub, the Royal Oak, was less than a hundred yards from the ground and that provided a convenient starting point. Thursday evening was official team night out, but I was available for any team that was going out any night. On Thursdays, everyone would bring a change of clothes to training so we could go straight out afterwards. On some nights, I failed to make it home at all. Then, I'd come to training in the clothes that I'd hit the town wearing. I have trained with a hangover more times than I can remember, but when you are young you think nothing of it.

On one of my birthdays, we started drinking at eleven in the morning in the garden of my house; by one o'clock in the afternoon, two people were upstairs asleep in a bedroom. We had played a drinking game involving Jack Daniels and they must have been caught out a few times. I suppose during the day we got through ten Jack Daniels each washed down with cans and cans of beer. We did some stupid things, like getting motorbikes out on the back field when we were drunk. The field was about two hundred yards long and it was possible to do jumps on the bikes. Often someone would be riding on the back seat – we took some daft risks. How nobody was seriously hurt I'll never know. We were like big kids showing off. At 7 p.m., we were ready to go out. When the taxis arrived, some of the lads tried getting in the boot. It seemed funny – you had to be there, I suppose. In the pub, vodkas were soon lined up on the bar.

It was that easy to be caught in the moment. You have the invincibility of youth. You can burn the candle at both ends without fear of harm, or so you tell yourself, and for a time you can. I was caught up in something I liked and didn't want to stop. The world started and ended with me, Jason Robinson, rugby player with a flash car and money to impress. I had made it into the first team; people were patting me on the back telling me how good I was. It is little wonder I began to feel invincible.

My head was stuck in the clouds – or the sand; it hardly matters which. I was getting great media coverage, I was wealthy by most people's standards, for some reason women found me attractive, I could do whatever I pleased. Undoubtedly, I got quite a lot of female attention during that time because I was a player with a famous and successful club. Had I been that bloke still working for Ultrasonic Cleaning Services, it would have been very different. Wigan was a rugby town and, by association, I was a star. At nineteen years old, I became an international.

You hope for things as you go through life; all of us do that, don't we? I hoped one day that I would play professional rugby. Then I hoped that I might win a trophy and I had done that in my first full season by being part of Wigan's Challenge Cup winning team. After that, I hoped I would be picked to play for my country. When it happened in 1993, it was an unrivalled feeling.

New Zealand were in England to play Great Britain in a three-Test series. The first was at Wembley, so once again I was able to taste the exhilaration of playing at the great stadium. Domestic rivalry is forgotten as the fans unite behind the British team. I was on the right wing, my Wigan team-mate Martin Offiah was on the left. The match could hardly have gone any better for the team or for me. I scored two tries in our 17–0 victory.

The first came from a cross-field kick from Shaun Edwards. The ball bounced in front of me as I was racing down the touchline. I had Sean Hoppe bearing down on me and, for all the world, it seemed as though the ball was heading into touch. But as it bounced – and it hardly got airborne – I scooped it in hand and, in the same motion, adjusted my body to jump over the line and squeeze in the corner before I was pushed into touch. My first try at Wembley – I could have done five cartwheels.

I have heard footballers describe how Wembley was a more tiring pitch than any other in the country, sapping the stamina like no other surface. Well, Central Park at Wigan was a big pitch so the size of Wembley was not a problem, but I can testify that playing there did take a physical toll. Perhaps the emotions attached to a big game – a Cup final or an international – drain you mentally and physically more than usual. The expectations of a crowd of almost 80,000 people could also be a factor. You do not want to fail.

After scoring once, a second try was a real bonus. Gary Connolly made a smart break down the right-hand side and the full-back was coming up on him. I was on his outside screaming, 'Kick it, kick it.' Gary managed to kick the ball between Hoppe and me, I won the race and went over the line again. I was named man of the match, which capped a debut that seemed scripted by a comic-strip writer. Well, I had already been christened Billy Whizz, after the character from *The Beano*.

But, like jockeys, racing drivers, skiers, boxers or footballers, rugby players are only ever one injury away from having their fantasies flattened. My flight of fantasy, when I was looking forward to warring with New Zealand in the second and third Tests, was grounded the very next weekend. I was tackled in the last minute of a match against Halifax; my arm was caught between two players and got pushed back the wrong way. I had dislocated my elbow – the hole in my elbow was big enough to stick a tennis ball in. The Test series with New Zealand was over for me. Happily, Great Britain won the series anyway.

Wigan were now playing under a new coach, John Dorahy. John Monie had left to take up an offer in Auckland, New Zealand. The 1993–94 season was to prove turbulent as a consequence. Dorahy's methods were at total odds with how we had worked under John Monie, and, let's face it, no one could accuse Wigan of under-achieving under him. In a winter of discontent, Dorahy lost the respect of the dressing room.

My own season turned sour before the Challenge Cup final with Leeds, a game that had such resonance for me having grown up in the city and been rejected by the club. Dorahy asked me to play in an A-team game to convince him I was ready to play in the final. We won and I was voted man of the match, but instead of making a decision then, he put me in the A-team again for a Tuesday night fixture in Cup final week. He said he just needed to see me again. I thought he was being economical with the truth and demanded that he be man enough to tell me that I was not going to play in the Cup final. Dorahy insisted I had a real chance of playing against Leeds, so dutifully I played for the A-team once more and I scored three tries. I had staked my claim with a vengeance, I thought, but when Dorahy listed his team for the final, my name was missing. I was steaming. I felt he had been dishonest. Had he told me that he didn't want to pick me, I could have taken it on the chin, but to have gone through the charade of playing two A-team games when he never had the remotest intention of playing me enraged me. I had been taken for a mug. Other players felt the same. Now it has never been a coach's job to win a popularity contest with his players; inevitably, he will make some unhappy by his team selections. But there has to be a degree of trust between players and a coach, a sense of fair play. I felt Dorahy had betrayed that principle. As a man I liked him, he was a nice guy. As a coach, I thought he fell short. I could have scored ten tries for the A-team and not been selected for the final. His mind had been made up before I played in those games.

As I say, others were similarly angry with Dorahy. Neil Cowie had been named on the travelling reserve list, but he told the coach he had no wish to accept the role, and Martin Hall was left out, too. Dorahy asked me to be a reserve. I told him, 'No chance.' As soon as the meeting was over, I headed for the snooker hall across the street from Central Park with some of my disgruntled team-mates. We were feeling bitter – and the more we drank, the more bitter we became.

Incensed, I rang the club chairman, Jack Robinson, no relation. It was a bold, some might say reckless, thing to do but I'd had a few beers and a few vodkas, and I no longer cared. I wanted him to know how unjust I felt it was that I had been left out of the final. I wanted him to hear my anger and unhappiness. I wanted him to know that I wanted to leave the club. It was the act of a young man whose anger had detached him from his senses. Mr Robinson listened, and told me that he would sort it out in due course. In the meantime, I went on a two-day bender before going down to Wembley on the coach that had been booked to take the staff to the final.

My place against Leeds had gone to Va'aiga 'Inga' Tuigamala – a man to whom one day I would owe an eternal debt of gratitude. Even though I knew it had nothing to do with Inga, there was still a sense that what had happened was personal. There was friction in the air, all generated by me.

I didn't enjoy the game, which we won 26–16 with tries from Offiah (two), Andy Farrell and Sam Panapa and five goals from Botica. I sat through it, but I didn't want to be there. I kept thinking that I should not have come down. My pride was hurt. The team was winning and they were winning without me.

The next day, we returned to Central Park for the traditional homecoming. I felt low so I disappeared straight into the changing room, and when I got there I found this big lump hammer. What it was doing there I have no idea, but it came in supremely handy. I picked it up and started to smash it against the walls. All the frustration and anger I felt was driving the hammer into the masonry with demented strength. I was mad and getting madder with each strike. Of course, I was doing all this in the name of tradition. Didn't Wigan players always trash the changing room after winning the Challenge Cup?

I wasn't alone. Cowie ran across the room and headbutted the false wall that divided the changing room from the corridor. His head went through the plasterboard and his ears got stuck, leaving him staring out into the corridor, unable to pull back in. We were in stitches – he looked like one of those trophies you see stuck above the fireplace in a country pub. Poor old Neil cut his ears as he finally escaped.

During another celebration – and I don't recall if it was this year or the following one after we beat Leeds again when I scored two tries and was awarded the Lance Todd Trophy – Offiah was hung from the top deck of the open-topped bus by his ankles. Let me explain: Martin was not a hard-drinking man, but he had been getting stuck into Coca-Cola with Bacardi. He may not have realised the amount of rum he was drinking, but after a while he was extremely sick. So, here was the most expensive player in the history of the English game, dangling upside down from the top of a bus driving through the streets of Wigan.

I do not believe anyone would question the professionalism of Wigan's players through the course of a season, but there were times when certain factions at the club ran out of control. To my knowledge, no one was hurt, but looking back I know that some of the stuff I did was downright stupid. It was all a question of joining the club, I think.

Dorahy never managed to join the club properly. His reign came to an end after the 1994 Challenge Cup final – and having been left out of the game, I cannot say I had an ounce of sympathy for his fate at that time.

Respect for John Monie had been unchallenged. If he said jump, you said, 'How high?' Dorahy made changes for the sake of change, or so it seemed to the players. Shaun Edwards is on record as saying:

Basically, John Dorahy tried to fix something that wasn't broken. When he first arrived, he came to see my dad and me and asked us to mark his card about the team and the club. Did John take the advice? No, he changed almost everything including things that didn't need changing at all. He would have us calling our old moves by new names for example. He changed most of the moves – even the ones we could rely on to work. He made training a real pain, the sessions were much longer and much more boring. We couldn't see the point. It wasn't as if we were doing badly when he arrived. Without sounding big-headed, I don't think he knew how to improve us, so instead of leaving us alone, he tried to control us.

Amanda, my beautiful wife and best friend, keeps my feet planted on the ground.

At three months old, the world looks very uncomplicated.

My first-ever official picture, taken when I started school.

On the beach at Cleethorpes with Carl Wilkinson, a boyhood friend from Leeds.

Proud captain of the Hunslet Boys Club Under-11 team; my best friend Damien Aleksic is on the far left of the front row.

Collecting the player of the year trophy at Hunslet Boys Club from local lad Garry Schofield, who had an outstanding career with Leeds and Great Britain.

On the break for Hunslet Parkside Under-13 team in a sevens competition at Leeds Rugby Club.

Retired scout Eric Hawley has special affection for this photograph of former Great Britain captain Ellery Hanley chasing me because he recommended us both to Wigan.

An early indication of the good times ahead at Wigan as I celebrate victory in the Academy final over Hull in May 1991.

Hanging out with my big brothers George and Bernard on the couch.

My boyhood friend Damien and I on our rental scooters on a Greek island. The adventure went wrong when Damien crashed trying to avoid a wandering donkey!

My first taste of being a winner at Wembley, crouching behind John Monie as we savour our triumph over Widnes in the 1993 Challenge Cup final.

Wigan team-mate Martin Offiah is the best rugby league winger I have seen, a one-off.

Apollo Perelini is catching up fast for great rivals St Helens. Off the field, we share a friendship that grew from being house-guests of John and Anne Strickland together. Later we joined up as team-mates at Sale.

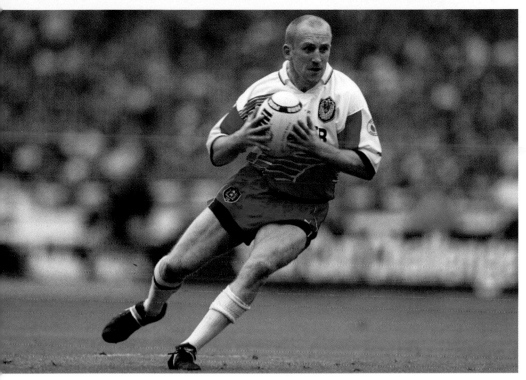

Shaun Edwards became an institution at Wigan – no elaboration needed.

I learned from Va'aiga Tuigamala, a true inspiration in my life, that happiness is unrelated to the car you drive or the money you have in the bank.

My granddad John Anderson, a lovely man, shares my pleasure at being awarded the Under-15 player of the year trophy at Hunslet Parkside.

With Nana Hilda at a family get-together.

I am the happiest man alive as I pose for a wedding-day portrait with Amanda at Tatton Hall on 21 November 1995. *Back row, left to right:* Roy (a friend of my mum's), Melanie (Amanda's sister) and my brothers Bernard and George; *front row, left to right:* Mum, David (Amanda's dad), us, Lynne (Amanda's mum) and Heather (Melanie's daughter).

Shaun was right – not much needed changing. One idea was to have us in at seven o'clock on Sunday morning. How ridiculous is that?

Jack Robinson must have realised there was a storm gathering. He knew there were some strong characters in the dressing room. He knew, too, the situation had to be resolved one way or the other. It seems the crunch came on the return journey from the Challenge Cup final. We pulled over at a service station and popular myth has it that Dorahy and the chairman scuffled as they were getting off the bus. I can honestly say I never saw it from where I was sitting, but Dorahy's days were over right then.

In *The Best Years of our Lives* by Paul Wilson, Robinson is quoted as remarking later:

> Once it became clear at the end of the season that the team would go down the tubes if we didn't sort out the situation, I acted quickly. That's what chairmen are for. It might sound brutal, but it is much easier to replace a coach than a dozen and a half world-class players. What had happened had to be John's fault. I dare say the players weren't blameless, but I couldn't very well sack them could I? Maybe we were partly at fault for recruiting the wrong man, I don't know. How do you go about finding the right person to deal with a dressing room full of world-class psychopaths? Every single coach to come down here has had grief from our players and some have nearly been broken by it. The only person who wasn't affected was John Monie, who was totally ruthless and wouldn't stand any nonsense. He actually terrified the players.

The chairman's thoughts never reached us at the time – we were merely grateful that the coach had been fired. With Dorahy history, Graeme West was appointed caretaker coach for the remainder of the season. West had worked in the club's pools office and coached the A-team from the time I joined the club. He was a former Wigan player and liked by everyone. I remember playing with him in the Alliance team; he was an old workhorse really.

West arrived with the first team in the nick of time to be in charge when we went to Brisbane to play the Broncos in the World Club Challenge. Under him, we were allowed to play the game we were used to playing.

The Broncos were the best team in Australia, and, to the Australian media, that meant they were the best team in the world. This was my first visit to Australia and the media there were different from what I had been accustomed to. All their reporting had an Australian bias. We had no chance. To read and listen to what was being said about us, we had wasted our time even boarding the plane from England.

Graeme West adopted a much more relaxed style of management than Dorahy's. He allowed us to go out on the town for three days after we arrived in Brisbane. Some of the guys went to nightclubs, some went to the casino. Often, they would return to the hotel by limousine, especially after a little win at the tables. Not much quality training was done because a lot of the players were worse for wear.

West's leniency was a strategic gamble. He figured if we had a good look at the local sights for a few days, we would be prepared to knuckle down for the remainder of the week leading to the game, and it worked. I can't say I got much sleep for those three nights; they were pretty wild. But then we dried out and focused on what we had come for – an important game of rugby against a club with a reputation to match that of Wigan. We did not want to have come all this way just to get walloped. I think the fear of being taken to the cleaners inspired us; that and the reaction we were getting in Australia. Everyone had written us off.

This time it was Tuigamala's turn to nurse disappointment. West chose me instead because it seems he was uncertain of Tuigamala's level of general fitness for what we knew was going to be a demanding game. West had the further disadvantage of not being able to select our best side. Kelvin Skerrett was in hospital at home with a broken jaw and Andy Platt had opted not to make himself available.

We were psychologically prepared for a physical game, and we had no intention of being intimidated by the Broncos before we even took the field – a fate that so many teams succumb to whenever they play an Australian side. We wanted to silence the 54,000 capacity crowd, who were in carnival mood after the organisers put on a huge fireworks display before the game. It was as though the Aussie party was in full swing before the game had even started. We responded by getting stuck in from the first whistle. We let the Broncos know we were not in the mood to take a backward step. It was not an evening for the squeamish, although it was a tough rather than dirty game. We won 20–14 and I provided one of the tries.

I picked up the ball after Michael Hancock dropped a pass. They told me later I went past four defenders, but it is hard to recollect the precise details. Instinct is at work at such moments. But I did hear what an Australian commentator said after I had crossed the line – 'Well, is he having a game or what? Jason Robinson will be mayor of Wigan!'

Thanks, mate! But the truth is that, as a team, we put on an amazing performance. It was a result few outside of our team felt could be achieved. Maybe the Broncos believed what was being said in the press and thought they had only to turn up to win. We showed them a lot of respect and maybe they did not have as much for us. Maybe that was the difference. We had flown to the other side of the world and beaten them in their back garden. I am sure it punctured their pride.

As for us, we didn't want to leave the stadium. We could have walked round for five hours if they had let us. That was the measure of the high we were on. Everyone went bananas that evening; it was one of the great nights for English rugby. Afterwards, West was given the coaching job on a full-time basis.

6

BORN AGAIN

'For God so loved the world that he gave his one and only son, that whoever believes in Him shall not perish but have eternal life.'

JOHN 3:16

My career was moving in a positive direction. After the success in Brisbane in the summer of 1994, we could look forward to the new season with much optimism. Sadly, I could not make the same claim for my life off the rugby field. It was a total mess.

I was in the middle of a mad social scene, I was young, had money in my pocket, a smart car and, by now, I was easily recognisable. I had sold my terraced house because once I had been given a sponsored car with my name written on the side, it seemed like a good idea to get away from a street where visiting fans parked for games. I moved into a detached house, not that far from the ground of Wigan Athletic FC. I had no need for decorators as I had bought the show home on the estate. I just walked in with my bags. I had all a young man could want, except, deep down, I had nothing.

It is astonishing how one relationship can change your life in an instant. It was daunting to be told one day that I was going to become a father. In so many ways, I was still a child myself. I had naively assumed that one day I would meet the right woman for me, grow together with her and then have children. The idea of fatherhood when I was barely twenty years old frightened me. I know that leaves me exposed to accusations of being irresponsible and I cannot properly defend the charge, except to say there are two sides to every story.

I vowed that I would be there for my child, but I knew that the relationship was never going to work. That was the only decision I made. I ran away from everything else.

To those on the outside, it appeared I had everything I could want. It is hard not to have your head turned in such circumstances. For a young man in my position, the adulation was like a drug – the more you have, the more you need. I could not deal with it. There was no one for me to turn to for advice, so my escape from this self-inflicted misery came at the bottom of a glass.

Having not had a father myself, I had been determined not to make the same mistake, but I had done just that. I was living a lie, like he must have done after getting my mum pregnant. I disliked what was happening, but I couldn't seem to do anything about it – except drink, that is. Each morning I'd wake up and be confronted by the reality of my situation. I just wanted to lose that feeling as soon as possible, so after training I would go for a drink. Soon it became a vicious circle – train, drink, sleep, awake to the ongoing nightmare, train and drink myself to sleep again. I was too immature to deal with the responsibility in any other fashion.

Then I met Amanda. She was working part-time in a menswear shop in Wigan while at college. On payday, I'd go in to town with some of the other lads and we'd go to the shop because we knew the owner.

I had first seen Amanda quite soon after I joined Wigan. Then I saw her much, much later in a supermarket queue and, still being painfully shy, I never spoke to her as much as I would have liked to have done. We never talked until I found her working in the menswear shop. Amanda has blonde hair, is very attractive, and I spent thousands of pounds on clothes I didn't need just because I wanted to go to see her. She was waiting for me to ask her out, I learned later, but I was in no position to start another relationship because of the problems I had to contend with already. I just chatted with her and I suppose I hoped something might come of it although I had no idea how I was going to make my troubles disappear.

Eventually, I gave Amanda a lift home from the shop. I remember meeting her mum and dad as I dropped her off, but I was too shy to look them in the eye. I really was as hopeless as that with most people.

After giving Amanda that initial lift home, we did start to see each other. I thought she knew about the fact that I was going to be a father because I had told the guy who owned the shop and assumed he had told Amanda. I was mistaken. It came out in conversation after we had been going out for two months. How did the news go down with Amanda? Like a lead balloon, actually. Thankfully, by the time my past caught up with me, Amanda said that she had fallen in love.

For me, however, the circle just became more vicious. I was still running from my problems, and that meant I was still getting drunk on a regular basis. I was naïve to suppose that when I was drunk I was invisible. You forget that in a small town like Wigan, when you play for the most successful club in the country, the reality is that nearly everybody knows you. Often Amanda stayed at my house, but I was still going out to pubs and clubs. Gradually, Amanda became unhappy with me going out and drinking excessively with some of the lads.

In October 1994, my son Lewis was born. I loved him from the moment I first saw him and I was determined to do my best for him, but fatherhood did not change the destructive cycle of my life. I was still on the town, still drinking heavily but still playing good rugby. Amanda and I split up, but after a couple of months, we started going out again. We went to nightclubs and we thought we were having a good time.

We'd not been back together for long when Amanda became pregnant. I now faced the prospect of having two children with two different women, to neither of whom I was married. I used to think about my own father and knew I was no better than him. I took full blame for what was happening. Under the circumstances, Amanda felt unable to stay. She went home to her parents, Lynne and David, and she also returned to God. Amanda had stopped going to church before I met her, but now she felt the need to draw strength from somewhere. She felt the need to get back on track.

Amanda was blessed to have good parents – even if her father *had* warned her, 'Don't get involved with rugby players.' Right now, I was in no position to argue with him.

This is how Amanda recalls that unhappy time, from her perspective:

From the beginning, my heart would pound if I saw him. I didn't watch him play – I didn't want to be like a groupie. Being from

Wigan, some of my family on my mum's side held rugby players in high esteem. I knew if I was going out with him that would please them! He was a good catch, but Jason was a very naïve nineteen year old, really.

I'd been very rebellious. When I first went to high school my mum sent me with two plaits in my hair, and wearing a brand new blazer, knee-high socks and a neatly fastened tie. My mum was very particular. I was intimidated by the older girls at school from day one. I was shocked and very naïve.

Basically, I am soft and I was so afraid what people might think of me. I changed my appearance in a hurry. By twelve years old, I knew that to be accepted I had to dress in a certain way and have a certain attitude. I didn't want to be perceived as a goodie-goodie because I was afraid of being ostracised. There was peer pressure to smoke, drink and have boyfriends at such a tender age. My parents were oblivious, initially.

The first they knew was at parents' evening at the end of my first year when they were informed by a teacher, 'Your daughter is no angel.' My mum was astounded. They had worked hard to give my sister and me the best they could. They had their own business and we had a lovely home. Sadly, the most important thing to me was what my friends thought. This was how the rebellion began.

Mum and Dad tried to rectify my behaviour. They moved me to a private school in the hope that this would work, but I never felt comfortable. I certainly didn't like the authority. At the school I met Mandy Woods, who befriended me, and through one of her friends I was introduced to an extraordinary church in Nottingham. Phyllis and Jim, her friend's parents, had been walking with the Lord for a long time. I always had a belief in God and when I was thirteen and off the rails, Phyllis and Jim sat me down in their house and prayed with me. The reality of their relationship with

God had an impact on me. They knew the Lord and had experiences of Him.

Their son took me to a church that they had previously belonged to in Nottingham, called the Congregation of Yahweh, which is the Hebrew name for God. I walked through the doors and felt a beautiful spirit in the room. There were lots of little Caribbean children and everyone was singing and clapping their hands or playing tambourines. It was apparent to me that these people knew their God. It wasn't happy-clappy, there was reality, a genuine belief, in that church. I knew God's spirit was there.

But I still did not have enough spiritual foundation to combat what was going on at school or in my social life, so I continued to go my own way and I reaped the consequences. It wasn't until the point of crisis that I returned to this church and to these people because I realised God was the only one who could help me.

I was still looking for something different and, in my early teenage years, I wanted to live in London. I wanted to have a good time. I had a cousin living there and I suppose I thought that was where it was really happening. My first step in that direction was moving to the nearest big city. At sixteen, I was living alone in Manchester, and very vulnerable. The next five years proved to be horrendous. At the end of them, I was desperately unhappy, and decided to go home.

I went back to the Congregation of Yahweh, and for some reason photographed the children there. Not long afterwards, I enrolled to study photography at night class in Wigan and I took the pictures with me. The lecturer encouraged me to pursue photography, so I began a course at college and found a part-time job in a menswear shop.

When Jason came in to the shop, I was stunned by how beautiful he was, but when he tried to impress me, he seemed young. I couldn't understand why he'd continually come in the shop on the days when I was working yet not bring himself to ask me out. I really liked him, but I wanted things to be right, so I waited and waited. It became ridiculous. I could only assume his shyness was stopping him from suggesting a date. Why else did he come specifically on the days I worked each week? My boss often said to me, 'Jason likes you a lot.' I couldn't make sense of the situation and my boss did not have an answer, either. Eventually, I asked Jason to give me a lift home.

We'd been seeing each other for two months and I was absolutely smitten. In a sense, I'd waited two and a half years to go out with him because I'd liked him from the moment I first saw him in town. He drove a BMW with a good sound system. At the time, those were the things that impressed me. I thought Jason was extremely attractive. I'd fallen in love.

He had a good job and I knew that my mum and dad wanted me to be with someone who would look after me. Jason was different; I thought everything was so positive. My dad's advice to me to have nothing to do with rugby players really irritated me. I thought he didn't understand. In my heart, I'd already decided and I was strong-willed.

I thought Jason was all I could hope for in a man, but then came the bombshell. We were at his house when he said something about a baby he was going to have. He could tell from my reaction that I did not have a clue about it. 'Didn't you know?' he asked. I sat in the reclining chair and had a cigarette – I don't smoke any more but I did then. I was in shock.

'Don't you think you should be with her?' I asked. Jason responded, 'I don't love her.'

I was trying to weigh it up in my mind. I wanted to have a clear conscience. I really liked him but I wanted things to be right. He explained the situation he was in and that helped me to understand. These things happen in life. Was I going to walk out on him now, the man I loved? I went to my mum and dad for advice. They told me it would be hard on me. Part of me questioned the sense of walking away from him. It is difficult to understand unless you have been in this position. After all, I loved him. Jason made it clear that he did not want to lose me and we continued to see one another. At twenty-one I was older than Jason and, in a way, I had grown up faster. I thought I could handle the situation, but I was not sure that Jason could.

He was the one in the centre of the storm. It was hard for me, never straightforward or comfortable. I felt on edge. It wasn't easy for Jason, either. Bearing in mind the childhood he'd had, he wanted to be there for his child more than anything. I respected that. But I had the feeling that he was putting this child before me because he felt guilty, and because his father had not been there for him. I suppose it was too sensitive an issue for him to want to address, but when you blank things out they are still there, buried deep. I could understand his feelings, but he couldn't find a balance and he shut me out, emotionally. That really hurt. I was angry and frustrated with the way he was handling it all. Jason was hung up. He kept all his feelings inside.

Then, less than three months after Jason's son was born, I discovered that I was pregnant. Part of me thought, 'I can't believe this,' but another part of me was glad. If you really love someone, surely it is natural that you want their baby. How did Jason react to the news? I think it was a big responsibility for an irresponsible young lad.

As I went on through the pregnancy, our relationship was strained. I heard rumours about him and told him that I did not want him to continue going out with the lads, but he did. He was adamant. I knew only too well what it was like out there and I needed him to settle down. I was heartbroken.

We'd been living together but I moved back to my mum and

dad's. I had all my stuff in the hallway and he just let me go. That said it all really. I knew I couldn't trust him any more.

I couldn't remember the last time I'd read my Bible, but out of the blue I picked it up again and turned to God. Deep down, I knew that one day I would return to God and now it was happening. I didn't want to carry on like we had been, and Jason wasn't husband and daddy material.

I said to God, 'Please show me the truth about this man,' and God answered my prayer. I was at a crossroads in my life. I was having a baby with the man I loved, but I felt so terribly insecure. Back living with my mum and dad, I started to go to church again. I remember as a child sitting on a swing and singing 'The Lord is my Shepherd' and I felt a presence. It was so real, I was frightened. My mum would have said she was a Christian at the time, but we never went to church, although I was sent to an All Saints school.

Before I left Jason's house, I asked him, 'What do you think will happen when you die?' Barriers came up immediately. He was defensive. He didn't want to consider things like that. He was just having a good time. Trying to get through to him was like banging your head against a wall. I thought if I carried on like that I would be going round in the same circles, never finding peace. I'd risk falling from one broken relationship into another with no sense of security and without plans for the future. I didn't want that for my baby and I didn't want it for me. I didn't want an environment of arguing and fighting. I could face that as a reality or I could put my life in God's hands and trust him to look after my baby and me.

Now I was back going to church with people whom I had known at thirteen. They were all supportive and prayed for me. There is a scripture that says as soon as you return to God, God will return to you. That's what happened to me.

As I went one way, Jason went another. Every so often I'd hear rumours and I struggled and tried to have a right heart towards him. It hurt deeply.

I suppose I had been tested because I knew I had to be right before God, that was the most important thing to me. On one particular occasion I was so distressed that I turned to my mum. I tried my best not to cry in front of her, but when I got to my bedroom I got on my knees and poured out my heart to God, and I waited on my knees for God's answer. There and then, he just showed me that Jason didn't know any better. As soon as God showed me that, it changed my heart towards Jason. Instead of hating him, I could pray for him. I could see he was lost.

It didn't stop me giving him a piece of my mind when I rang him. One time I remember I said, 'It's not just women's lives you're messing about with, it's the lives of children.' I could hear Jason crying. I'd never been able to get through before so *something* must have happened. I also told him that as he had a good job, it was unfair to expect my mum and dad to pay for the cot and pram and everything else our baby would need. I thought he could take some responsibility for the baby. Not that long afterwards, he sent me a parcel and it included my Bible, the one that I'd left at his house. Also in the package was money for the cot and pram, the amount I'd said I needed. In the front of the Bible he'd written, 'I am now born again. If you need me for anything I am here.'

I was overwhelmed. I thought my prayers had been answered but I was still scarred. I had been very hurt and I had a baby to think about. Again, I went to my mum to see what she thought. Basically, she said I should have nothing to do with him. In fact, both my parents told me not to bother with him. I was in a difficult position. I still loved him and I was carrying his baby. I thought, 'What if he *has* changed? What if he really is born again?' All trust had been destroyed between us, yet my heart's desire was that he should become a good husband and daddy. So I prayed and all I could get from God was 'You've just got to trust me.'

I rang Jason and said I'd talk. He was living temporarily with John and Anne Strickland, Christians whom he had met through Inga. Ultimately, I had to trust God because you don't really know what is in someone's head and heart. I explained all this to my mum and dad. I was in a dilemma – it was too important not to give our relationship a chance, yet with a baby involved it was too important to make a wrong decision.

I had always imagined the father would be present at the birth of my baby, and Jason was there when Cameron was born. Jason said it was a miracle that I allowed it. Even before Cameron arrived on 8 September 1995, he sent three bouquets of my favourite flowers, sunflowers, lilies and red roses. I had a horrendous time. I thought I was going to die in childbirth, and Jason's presence really bonded us.

He went back to his house to live. My conscience wouldn't agree to him living with us at my parents' home because we weren't married and I was now a committed Christian. God had blessed me and looked after me and there was no way I was going to violate God's laws like I had before. I knew there was no other way for me to live.

Jason respected that but he hated being alone. He desperately wanted to be with me, but at the forefront of my mind was the scripture that says, 'Honour God and He will honour you.' By this time, I had learned to respect God. I was thinking about Psalm 37: 'Delight thou also in the Lord and he shall give thee thy heart's desire. Commit thy way unto the Lord, and put thy trust in him and he shall bring it to pass.'

I got my engagement ring out again – we had been engaged – and put it on. I told my parents that we wanted to get married as soon as possible. I really loved Jason. Now I wanted to do things

God's way, according to his will, and not on my own, because this had only brought heartache.

You can see from Amanda's story that I was in emotional free fall. One minute I was a young lad with the world at my feet, then I was in this ever-deepening black hole. Still, I kept drinking as a means to escape.

But through the fog of my own despair, I could not help but notice Va'aiga Tuigamala. This big man from Western Samoa was to prove the starting point of my salvation. In Inga I saw a man who was always happy. I had looked for happiness from relationships, from cars, from alcohol, but nothing so far had fulfilled what I was searching for. I might be happy for a week, for two weeks, but it never lasted. I was chasing material things – a bigger house, a nicer car. I was never satisfied. Inga wasn't chasing anything. He didn't go out drinking with the lads. He didn't sleep around. He didn't have the best car in the car park. Why was he so happy?

Sometimes you'd go into the treatment room and find Inga reading the Bible. He would read aloud. Clearly, this meant so much to him. We talked together. I asked some simple questions, and he gave me some straightforward answers. As a born again Christian he had placed his life in the hands of God and that was the source of his contentment. He knew I had problems, but he never tried to force any details from me and he never tried to convert me to Christianity. For my part, I was not prepared to open up too much. I had always had trouble expressing my feelings. I kept everything inside.

I didn't need to hear too many words from Inga. What impressed me was the way he lived. To see him full of joy each morning when he came into the club was revealing. He was the only person I knew who genuinely enjoyed his life.

One morning Inga arrived for training and made a beeline for me. He wanted an urgent chat. 'I had a dream about you last night,' he explained. In his dream, I was stood on top of the world. Metaphorically, that's where I was in my life; my career was going from strength to strength. But in his dream, Inga watched the world begin to crumble under my feet. That was my life off the pitch. Things were crumbling all around me.

I cannot tell you how blind I'd been. What more needed to happen for me to realise how morally bankrupt and shallow my life really was? Suddenly, with the dawning of the light from Inga's dream, I saw what I really wanted, the things money could not buy – a loving family, inner peace and the capacity to live a good moral life. I realised I wanted to enjoy my life, full stop. As long as I kept running from my personal problems, I was kidding myself. The people around me in the team and in the pubs and clubs were happy to take me at face value. I was sheltered from reality. Amanda had seen through the façade. She had been up close and there were aspects of my life that could not withstand that kind of scrutiny. Amanda saw a man she could no longer tolerate. She would call me on the phone and tell me how bad I was. She tried to open my eyes to my responsibilities; basically, she got into my ribs. Amanda vented the frustration that was consuming her, but I was cocooned in my own world.

Then one night I listened to her arguments with an open rather than a shut mind. For the first time, I realised she had a point. She told me my behaviour was unacceptable, that I was hurting people, and this message started to unscramble my thoughts. She was angry – as she was entitled to be – but her voice was controlled and calm. She called because she cared. She was having my baby, but she could not consider living with me the way I was. I didn't want to believe what she said was true – who would? Yet I could see with new-found clarity what I had done and I really didn't like what I saw. I told myself the real me was not how I was being perceived, but I could only convince others by changing my lifestyle.

Amanda's anger and frustration eroded my usual defences, her words hurt and sobered me. At last I understood how out of order I had been. I couldn't go on like this another day. I needed a new beginning. I was no longer blind and, as it says in the Bible, I felt like God had taken the scales from my eyes.

When I got off the phone I just sobbed and sobbed. Partly out of self-pity, but mostly through regret at the pain I had caused. I wanted to change – yet how? In a drawer in my kitchen I had a set of knives that were a present from my mum when I moved into the house. One of them was a cleaver. Well, I took it from the set and held it in my hand. I just felt so low. I thought, I really can't go on like this, can't cope with more heartache. I can't say I was going to take my life, but I sat there, with the knife in my hand, considering the problems I faced, and thought I could end all the misery. But deep inside I knew there had to be another answer and I put the knife away.

The tears did not dry up. I knew there had to be more to my existence than playing rugby and going out and getting drunk night after night. There had to be a greater reason for being on this earth than that, surely. I didn't want to depend on material things to make me happy. The young man who had been living like this wasn't the real me. I was still crying when

I finally fell asleep, long after Amanda had hung up the phone.

When I awoke, I called John Strickland. I had been introduced to him and his wife Anne through Inga. They had their own office in town and offered to see me straightaway. I had bought a convertible, to be seen in, I suppose; but on this morning, for the first time in my life, I did not want to be seen. However, I drove to their office and when I had parked, I reported to reception. I must have looked an awful state. My eyes were puffed and red because I had had so little sleep. Doubtless I looked rough but, if I did, John and Anne were too polite to dwell on my appearance. Once in their office, they realised I had problems I was no longer capable of handling. They were Christians living a Christian life and that was why I had gone to see them. Besides, Inga had shown me there was another way to approach life and that was his gift to me.

With John and Anne, I felt I could unburden myself; and I suspected they would listen without being judgemental. From the moment I sat down, John said, 'When you leave here this morning, you will have a smile on your face.' I said nothing. I was still feeling so low – you cannot get any lower than entertaining a thought to take your own life. John and Anne talked and listened and asked me, 'Do you want to ask Jesus into your life?'

'Yes,' I replied.

Right there, I asked God for forgiveness. The three of us prayed together and I asked him to come into my heart. Although I didn't fully understand what I was doing at that point, I knew it was what I wanted. John and Anne told me God could help me and I wanted his help. I didn't know what was going to happen, but I was convinced it would lead me to another way of life. What God showed me was clear and concise – 'Look, you've got everything that you thought would make you happy and yet you are still unhappy. Now will you follow me?' I was ready to make the commitment.

Nevertheless, I still had reason to be sceptical about leaving John and Anne with 'a smile on my face'. I had got into trouble with the police while out drinking and, after thanking John and Anne for their kindness, I left to keep an appointment with my solicitor. Hanging over my head were charges of assault, affray and criminal damage.

At the beginning of July 1995, I'd had a weekend away at a hotel in Bridlington with some of my family and friends. Late in the evening a fracas started after some lads came back from a night out. Police were called to the hotel, and when they came the next day my brother George and I were cautioned, placed under arrest and briefly locked in a cell.

Regrettably, matters worsened. Due to a misunderstanding, I failed to appear before magistrates at Bridlington as I was supposed to do on 22 September. The next morning the *Hull Daily Mail* ran a story under the headline: 'Arrest him! Court acts after rugby league star fails to appear'. It revealed that magistrates were planning to issue a warrant for my arrest, and another one for George. The story read:

> Rugby League superstar Jason Robinson is facing arrest for failing to answer an assault charge for the second time. Fed-up magistrates ordered the sporting hero to be detained when he failed to attend Bridlington Court yesterday. The 21-year-old Great Britain and Wigan ace Robinson is set to be arrested on a warrant not

backed by bail. Magistrates issued warrants for the arrest of Robinson and his brother, George Brannan (25), who also failed to turn up.

Imagine the panic! News of the warrant for my arrest was broadcast on television, too. I was in hiding. I called Wigan and asked for a parking space to be left as close as possible to the front door for the next game. Wigan's executives were not in the dark about the fracas in Bridlington. Once he had heard the details of what had taken place at the hotel, Jack Robinson pledged the club's support. The truth was I failed to appear in court for one simple reason — I did not know I was expected to be there. I had always intended to go to the court to defend myself.

Frantic calls to the court from my legal advisors resulted in the warrant for my arrest being hurriedly withdrawn. My solicitor, Keith Parks, told the *Hull Daily Mail* for publication on 25 September: 'I have spoken to Bridlington Magistrates' Court this morning and there has been a mix-up which is now being unravelled. The arrest warrant will be officially withdrawn today and we expect a new date to be set for the hearing.'

Finally, the court hearing took place on 14 November. Television and newspaper cameramen trailed me down the street on my way to the court entrance. Jack Robinson was present to support me. With George, I pleaded guilty to using threatening behaviour at the hotel but pleaded in mitigation that we had faced provocation. The court was also told how Mum had suffered a fractured cheekbone. They also heard that since the incident had taken place, I had given my life to the Lord.

In the circumstances, the magistrates gave both George and

me a twelve-month conditional discharge and ordered us to pay prosecution costs of £50 each. While glad the ordeal had ended, I still felt a sense of injustice. But I had learned a hard lesson. I would no longer go to pubs or clubs because you are exposed to unwanted trouble.

7

TAKING OUR VOWS

'Therefore a man shall leave his father and his mother,
and shall cleave unto his wife and they shall be one flesh.'

GENESIS 2:24,25

John and Anne invited me to live with them for a while, as I
tried for a better and happier life. They had missionaries and
pastors staying with them, and they felt I could benefit from
the fellowship. We had prayer meetings and Bible readings; it
was an introduction course for me. I needed to be in the
company of people who were not going to take me the wrong
way. I needed to withdraw from what I had been doing in order
to learn to live this new life. I needed to discover more about
Christianity. The word means being Christ-like and that's how
I wanted to be. If I had stayed in my old environment, there
was a real chance I would have drifted back into my old ways.

I told my mates in the team that I would no longer be available for a night out, and I meant never again. 'Sure, Jason,' they
said, not believing a word of it. They thought I'd get over it in
a week, two at most.

Martin Hall was one of my closest friends in the dressing
room until he left Wigan in 1998. Here's how he tells it:

I remember the last time I went out with Jason. It was a bank holiday Monday in 1995 and we had played St Helens. We went on to Leeds, then Wakefield. I had seen him changing. I felt a lot was going on in his mind. He had moved in with some people who were changing the way he lived. That was his choice. I'm a Catholic, not a practising one, but I do believe in God.

I knew he was low. Jason, Kelvin Skerrett, Neil Cowie and I were close. We played rugby, went out for a pint, and had chats. After all, as full-time players we had lots of free time. I understood Jason had some tough things going on in his life with girlfriends.

Of course, it was still strange when Jason made such a drastic change. After he said he wasn't coming out any more, he had the mickey taken out of him but it was only the normal banter you get in a dressing room. We expected him to be his old self after a week or two. Even though he was reserved, he was always up for a night out.

After training almost every Thursday we would go out as we didn't have another session until Saturday morning. We'd go round Wigan and finish at a nightclub called the Turnkey. Nine times out of ten I'd stay at Jason's house. Other nights, Jason would go over to Wakefield. He had so much time on his hands and he was single. He was paid reasonably well and he probably could handle going out more often than some of us! We were a bit wild on occasions, but we made sure we always performed on the pitch for Wigan. We trained hard and played hard.

When Jason didn't come out with us again, I thought, 'Good luck.' We had some great days when drinking and going out was part of the culture of the game. It's not that long ago, but times change and it would not be possible to do that today. The game has got that much quicker.

My mates at Wigan may have been able to handle the situation, but I couldn't and I needed help. It was simply that I didn't want to live like that any more. By living in Anne and John's house, which was also home to Apollo and Selina Perelini, I abandoned that lifestyle. Apollo, a Samoan-born loose forward, was playing for St Helens and we shared the top floor of the house. Selina cooked for me, a helpless bachelor, and really looked after me. It was good for me to have young people like them around, who were grounded in the faith. Rugby fans might be amused to learn that on days when Wigan and Saints were playing against one another – and rivalries didn't come any bigger in rugby league – Selina would prepare pre-match meals for both of us. I trusted her not to give me food poisoning! Later, we built an even stronger friendship when Apollo signed for Sale at the same time as I did.

Of course, there were occasions when I had a conscience about not being with the lads and I thought I could go out and not drink. I was kidding myself. I tried taking my car, thinking that would stop me from drinking – still fooling myself. All that happened on those nights was that I'd have a couple of drinks, and give my car keys to someone else so they could drive it home. I'd end up having a skinful again. This was a self-defeating exercise. One day in that summer of 1995 I was browsing through a daily reading book and realised that, in essence, it way saying you can't sit on the fence; either you go your way through life, or you go God's way. From that moment, I never took an alcoholic drink in a pub again.

It was a special moment to see Amanda bring our child into the world. I am not good at showing emotions, but I confess to having a lump in my throat. Seeing your child born is an amazing experience, one that you will never forget.

Emotionally, I am not always able to express myself as I would like. If only Amanda could see the love I have for her, if she could see my heart, hear the words I would like to say, she would be so much reassured. There is a barrier I am constantly trying to get through. Sometimes, I leap through it. Sometimes, I cannot even step up to it. It is a slow process, but with patience, I think I'm making progress.

When Amanda and Cameron came home, I spent nearly all my time at her parents' house. David and Lynne had the room because they had built an extension, and it was important for them to see us all together. If you've hurt a man's daughter, you have to live with your tail between your legs for a long time. Thankfully, they gave me another chance because Amanda had said that was what she wanted. After we were married, it was an important decision to live with Amanda's parents, I believe. I needed to be in the right environment and this was the place for us to be together. I had to win back everyone's trust, not just Amanda's. It took a long time for the scars to heal, but slowly they did.

We were married on 21 November 1995 at Tatton Park. We had the service there rather than in a church because we are non-denominational. By restricting the guestlist to twenty people there were those in the family who felt disappointed not to have been invited. All the arrangements were very rushed, but we just wanted to get married. Amanda says we'd probably do it differently now, but the main purpose of the wedding was to make a commitment to each other. We knew that we had done things the wrong way round; we wanted to make things right.

As it was in the rugby season, our honeymoon was a few snatched days together. We spent our wedding night in

Manchester, then took a suite at the Savoy Hotel in London for two nights.

After all we had been through, Amanda, Cameron and I had become a family in the eyes of God and the law. I could not have been happier.

8

FAREWELL
CENTRAL PARK

'The better you become the more people will try to find
something wrong with you.'

ROBERT LANSDORP.

My mum has to be the only Wigan fan living in Leeds. She
used to have plenty to say down at her local club when we won,
so you can guess what she was like the day I ran in five tries
for Wigan against Leeds at Central Park in 1996. I had never
scored five in one match before – and it was extra special to
establish that record against Leeds, my home-town club.

I had begun to get stronger and the things that used to
swallow me up no longer had the same effect. My new lifestyle
meant giving up a lot of things and, early on, I didn't give up
as much as I should have done.

I think I was still playing well. In the 1997 internationals
against Australia, I was nominated man of the series; and I won
the same award against New Zealand in 1998. Great Britain
just fell short in both series, which was a shame because that
seemed always to be the case. I love playing for my country.

When I made my debut for Britain in 1993, the players were jumping out of their skins to seize the opportunity, but that was no longer the case by 1997, in my opinion. Players who did so well at club level seemed to withdraw into their shell when it came to international rugby. I don't know if they felt the pressure or whether it was a reflection of their inexperience, but it happened to so many players. I always thought we had a team to beat Australia and New Zealand – never had a doubt – but it never happened. We always seemed to take a backward step at some point in the series. One of the problems was that we did not play that many internationals. We'd either play the Australians or New Zealanders here, or get on a plane and go over there. Either way, we did not have much time to prepare. You can't go from club level to playing against the world's best. It just doesn't work like that. You need games to bring players through. By the end of the 1998 series, I thought it less likely that we would ever win.

By 1998, John Monie had returned to coach Wigan. He was surprised by what he found. He says, 'When I went back they hadn't won anything for a while and I discovered they had forgotten the good habits and the hard work that it takes to be a great team.' He also saw a change in me:

> Jason's attitude to the game had not changed, he was still ruthless, still knew what he wanted. He knew how he wanted to play and my job as a coach was to give him a bit of guidance in that area. But he had his personal life in order. A lot of tough players turn out to have a soft side to them and they don't mind showing it. He had turned everything around.
>
> Sure, players still went for a drink. That happens at most football clubs, no matter what code. They'd had coaches who went

with them to the pub, but I was not in that mould. I always went home when it was over. They stood around with their mouths open for six months, thinking, 'When's the coach going to come out with us?' Maybe Jason had to tell them I wasn't coming out with them. I was just business.

For Wigan – now Wigan Warriors – the 1998 season climaxed with the inaugural JJB Super League Grand Final against Leeds Rhinos at Old Trafford on 24 October. It was a Saturday evening and it was raining. As a team that likes to pass the ball, we would have preferred it to be dry; but a rainy night in Manchester would have to do. One Monie-ism seemed apt for the occasion: 'All it takes is all you've got'. John always liked to decorate the dressing room with messages. Another of his favourites was: 'Individuals play games and teams win championships'. At Wigan, we were always strong on teamwork.

Leeds, though, set the pace when Richie Blackmore scored the opening try. We spent most of the half on the back foot until the moment that the BBC would later call the try of the season. I received the ball on the right touchline in the thirty-seventh minute, and ran across the line of Leeds defenders, looking for a gap I could exploit. The defence was coming at me but I managed to step outside one man, and inside another. I was free and I knew it, so I ran straight for the posts and dived between them. It happened in a flash; one second I was confronted by a wall of Leeds players, the next I was in the clear. It must have been galling for them, especially as Andy Farrell kicked the conversion and then a penalty to give us an 8–4 lead at half-time. Leeds had played the better rugby, but I know which dressing room was happier during the interval.

The second half was just as tight, the only additional score being another penalty by Andy. I have probably scored better tries than that one, but don't they say timing is everything in life? With it being the inaugural Grand Final, there was so much hype surrounding the game. To score that try just before half-time gave the team a psychological edge. At the end, I carried Cameron with me as I went to collect my commemorative ring. On the pitch, Andy was asked by a television reporter what it was like to have won under this new format. 'I am absolutely exhausted,' he said. 'If this is what Grand Final football is about, I want to be in it every year. All season comes down to this . . . you have to be desperate to win . . . this one's for everybody at the club.'

I knew what he meant. I was being hailed for my try, and the funny thing with sport is that everybody wants to be associated with those who steal the headlines. All the praise is reserved for the guy who pulls something out of the bag and, on this occasion, it was me. I won the Harry Sunderland Man of the Match Trophy, making me the only player to have received that award and the Lance Todd Trophy, which is given to the man of the match in the Challenge Cup final. But what about the others? What about the forwards who are smashing into one another to win the ball for a guy like me. They get the rough end of the stick, but their contribution is immense to any winning effort.

We all have different talents. Mine is something I enjoy doing and it's my job. Perhaps people look at me with higher regard than they do others because of all the hype. I mean, don't tell me what we do is more important than what nurses, firemen and the police do every day. It is just that sportsmen and women are in the public eye. Like it or not, we are thought of as role models. I am glad that I managed to sort things out because I believe I am now a more positive role model than I was before. I feel I can show people that you don't have to follow the crowd; you don't have to be a sheep and do what everybody else is doing. There is another way. It's not all bright lights.

After winning the Grand Final, the Wigan team was broken up to the distress of all concerned. Some players left, others were forced out. John Monie explained that we were paying a fine every month for breaking the salary cap, so we had to drop around twelve players from the squad. He was not happy about it and told the directors at the time that if there were injuries to key players, we were going to be in trouble. After the first few games of the next season, six or seven injured players ended up sitting in the stand because we played pretty tough. John told me he was having a bit of trouble with the chairman, Peter Norbury. The club was gearing up to finish at Central Park and move to the JJB Stadium. They were letting the place run down. It was dirty, the showers were dirty, and the pitch wasn't looked after. John and the chairman were at each other most weeks, which was making John's job unpleasant. You can trace the decline of the great days from around then.

We were training here, there and everywhere – sometimes at schools, sometimes on the top pitch at Central Park. When you thought how much the players were worth, it was a joke, what was happening, but none of us was laughing. We had to pull bricks out of the ground before we could train. We dug up enough bricks to build the new stadium. It was hardly a professional environment for professional athletes to go to work.

I think the lid blew off after Castleford beat us in a close

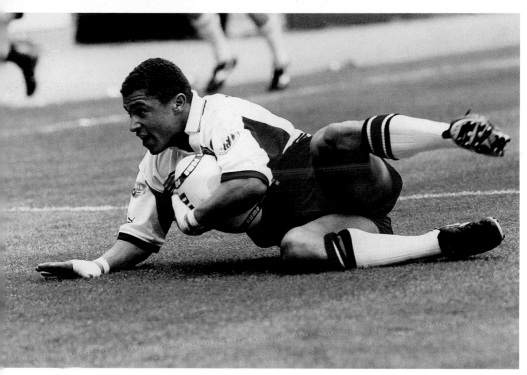

appear a picture of serenity as I ground the ball for the first of my two tries for Wigan against Leeds in the 1995 Challenge Cup final...

..but I soon shatter that illusion as I release a primal scream in celebration with Shaun Edwards and Lee Jackson...

...but I recover my composure in time to offer a prayer of thanks on the side of the Wembley pitch.

Holding the Lance Todd Trophy, which I wa awarded as player of the match in that 1995 final.

Embracing Frano Botica after my second try against Leeds, before he made the successful conversion.

My momentum takes me over the try line for England in the opening pool game against Australia at Wembley in the 1995 Rugby League World Cup.

Australia had the last word – Andrew Johns, ball in hand, was one of their key players as they beat England in the World Cup final.

Captain Andy Farrell and I resting easy on the Super League Grand Final Trophy, which Wigan won in 1998.

I received the Harry Sunderland Trophy for my performance in that Grand Final.

I can see only the line as I burst through the Leeds defence to score a critical try in the Grand Final.

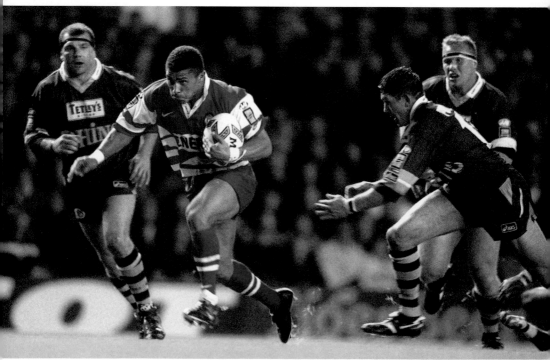

My momentum takes me over the try line for England in the opening pool game against Australia at Wembley in the 1995 Rugby League World Cup.

Australia had the last word – Andrew Johns, ball in hand, was one of their key players as they beat England in the World Cup final.

On a collision course with history – in 1996 Wigan became the first rugby league team to be invited to play in the Middlesex Sevens at Twickenham, the headquarters of rugby union, of course.

Momentously, we won (I'm seated on the far left of the front row).

At Maine Road in early May 1996, Wigan showed union guys that we could play rugby when we defeated Bath 82–6. The game was played under league rules.

Later that month, Bath took revenge, beating us 44–19 at Twickenham under union rules. Jon Sleightholme sprints out of my reach.

Captain Andy Farrell and I resting easy on the Super League Grand Final Trophy, which Wigan won in 1998.

I received the Harry Sunderland Trophy for my performance in that Grand Final.

I can see only the line as I burst through the Leeds defence to score a critical try in the Grand Final.

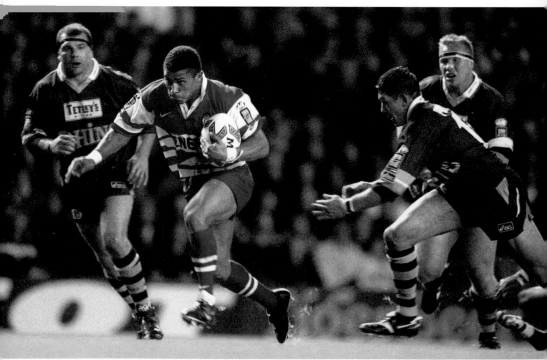

Fans strolling away from Central Park for the last time, 5 September 1999, after Wigan's poignant win over Saints, a day that brought a lump to my throat.

Kris Radlinski shares the end of the bitter-sweet last afternoon at Central Park, the home of Wigan for 96 years, 364 days.

Chaired from the pitch by Andy Farrell (*left*) and Dennis Betts after my last home game for Wigan at the new JJB Stadium in October 2000.

Left Jonathan Davies, in action for Wales in the 1995 Rugby League World Cup, made the opposite journey to me, swapping codes at a time when union was an amateur game.

Below I first tried rugby union in the winter of 1996, when I was contracted to Bath in the league off-season. Here, I am targeted by Cardiff and Wales scrum-half Rob Howley in a European Cup quarter-final.

game at Central Park. Everyone came into the dressing room deeply disappointed. In moments like that, players need time to get over what has happened. Everyone was just sat there, heads down, wishing 'if only . . .'

Suddenly, the door burst open and Peter Norbury stormed in. He said something like, 'I need a meeting, something is wrong,' and started having a go at us. Fair play to John, he cut in. He was not having the chairman talking to the players when they had just left the pitch, beaten and downhearted. It's the last thing you expect from a chairman – but he was new to his role and he didn't understand. If the directors have a problem, they go to the coach. The coach is the one who has to sort it out. He and John had a row right there in front of all the players. Then one of the front rowers got the chairman by the arm and walked him to the door, saying that he was out of order and shouldn't have come in. John told us not to worry about it. We just had to play, he would coach and Peter Norbury should be the administrator.

We tried to put it behind us, but John was sacked a couple of weeks later. His second spell at the club had lasted a season and a third. Later, when former chairman Maurice Lindsay came back to get the club out of the mess it had got into, he offered John his job back, but he turned it down. John played an important part in my development as a player and I was going to miss him.

Another era came to an end with the closure of Central Park on 5 September 1999 – 96 years and 364 days after the first game at the ground; the 18,179 tickets were sold out weeks in advance for Wigan's final game against St Helens. It was an emotional day for many of us. Central Park had a hold on me.

I had first played at the ground in 1991 and it was home. To play the last game against our archrivals made the occasion all the more poignant. We dare not lose. Had we done so, St Helens would have been gloating for the next hundred years. To understand the depth of feeling between Wigan and St Helens, consider the fact that Gary Connolly was transferred from Saints to Wigan as long ago as 1994. To my knowledge, to this day he is still called Judas in St Helens.

To be honest, Central Park was from another age. The facilities for the fans were not that good, but that was to miss the point. The place smelled of history. People could walk to the ground because of its central position in town. Fans would have a drink and mingle with friends they had known for years and years. There was a homeliness about the place.

In the dressing room before the final game, I could sense that those who had been at the club for a long time were feeling as emotional as I was. Andy Farrell, Kris Radlinski and Gary Connolly knew the significance of the match we were about to play. At Central Park, a man had his own place in that dressing room. If you were a young newcomer and sat in the wrong place, you'd find your clothes in a heap in the middle of the floor.

I just knew we were going to win. It seemed as though we were playing for the whole town, and all the players past and present. We didn't want to be remembered as the last Wigan team to play at Central Park who lost to St Helens.

My mum had come over from Leeds, as had an uncle of mine, and Amanda, her parents, her sister, nan and niece were there. It was a big family affair. This game would not pass unheralded into the mists of history. We won 28–20, I scored two tries and won man of the match, and the crowd went bananas. At the end, it was as though we had won the World Cup. We just walked and walked round the ground with the fans singing and chanting and making enough noise to be heard in Manchester. Brilliant, unforgettable. Later, as I walked back to our car, Amanda took a picture of me in front of the ground. I had a lump in my throat. I have not had many days like that.

This seems an appropriate place to speculate about the best Wigan team I played in. I loved playing in all of them, and any selection is guaranteed to upset someone. Everyone I played alongside at Wigan should know it was a privilege to be in the same team as them.

Front row: Andy Platt, Martin Dermott, Kelvin Skerrett. Back three: Denis Betts, Phil Clarke, Andy Farrell. Scrum-half: Shaun Edwards. Stand-off: Frano Botica (for his kicking brilliance, but it was a close call with Henry Paul and Tony Smith). Left wing: Martin Offiah. Right wing: Jason Robinson. Centres: Gary Connolly and Dean Bell (sub, Va'aiga Tuigamala). Full-back: Kris Radlinski (for the last couple of years, the best performer in Super League).

That last game at Central Park was joyful for the way we had played and won, and it was sad because it signified the passing of all that history. For years, as you drove into town you saw the big red stands of the old stadium, important as a symbol of what Wigan stood for. Seems funny when you pass it now. It's just a supermarket. It's like the heart has been ripped out of the town.

9

AUSSIE RULES – ALMOST

'When an archer misses the mark, he turns and looks for the fault within himself; failure to hit the bullseye is never the fault of the target. To improve your aim improve yourself.'

GILBERT ARKLAND

Having been left out of the Challenge Cup final the previous season, imagine how miserable I felt when I was injured a couple of weeks prior to the 1995 final. I broke a bone in my hand and a bone in my foot, but I was determined not to miss out again – a mood heightened because Wigan were to meet Leeds. Any player will tell you they want to do well against their home-town club and I was no exception.

Throughout the countdown to the Cup final I was considered 'doubtful' to make it on to the Wembley pitch, but after consultation between the coaching staff, the medical team and me, it was felt I could take the risk of starting. What they had not told me was the amount of pain I would experience from the 'pain-killing' injection I needed in my right foot. My damaged hand was padded in an attempt to protect it from further injury, but it was my foot that was more seriously hurt. The soreness had not gone away since the injury occurred.

The injection was delayed until close to kick-off time. If I had not been held down in the dressing room, I would have gone through the ceiling. The pain as the needle passed through into the base of my foot was excruciating. Afterwards it seemed a small price to pay to get me on to the pitch, as I so badly wanted to play against Leeds, the club who chose not to sign me. The great thing was the injection worked to the point where I couldn't feel a thing; it was like having only one leg.

As usual, the scene that greeted us as we took the field was amazing. The stadium was a carnival of colour and noise. In the moments before kick-off, the sense of occasion hits you like a sledgehammer. For the next eighty minutes you know your body is going to be on the line. There is no chance to make amends another day. If you win, you go home with the Cup. If you lose . . . well, you don't think about losing. These are the days you dreamed of as a kid, when you tucked the ball under your arm and ran like the wind and fantasised that you were diving under the posts at Wembley. Losing is not an option. This is what you tell yourself and this is what you believe.

In the event, the final on that afternoon of 29 April was not two minutes old when Graham Holroyd kicked a penalty goal for Leeds. But this was to prove Wigan's day – my day. My leg was to hold up better than I dared hope. I ran almost forty metres to score the first try of the final. I remember breaking clean from the Leeds defence, then having full-back Alan Tait to beat. I had been given too much room on the outside and I took it. I was never going to be caught and, cheekily I concede,

I blew a kiss to the crowd before touching the ball down. You've heard this before, but I was over the moon.

Kelvin Skerrett, Neil Cowie and Martin Hall punched holes all over the pitch as the game unfolded. My second try came four minutes after half-time when I took possession at a play-the-ball. Sometimes, you just get on a roll and that was what happened. I beat some of the Leeds forwards who were ambling back, and there was nobody around to touch me. After Frano Botica kicked the conversion, the scoreboard read Wigan 18 Leeds 2. Our supremacy was never going to be challenged from that point.

Strong running from Va'aiga Tuigamala was a constant threat to Leeds. Often three players were needed to halt Inga's progress. There was an inevitability that Inga would score a try, as did Henry Paul and Hall, while Botica kicked five goals. Critics hailed us for playing inventive, breathtaking open rugby as we won the game 30–10. For an eighth successive year, the Cup belonged to Wigan. I was awarded the Lance Todd Trophy after being named man of the match. Winning was reward enough, but having been deemed a doubtful starter until the very last moment, this final will always have a special place in my memories.

It was a big year in my life in so many ways. I became a Christian, I became a father for a second time, I married and I stopped drinking. Before all these things happened, I also signed a contract to play in Australia and I appeared for Great Britain in the rugby league World Cup final.

I was never aware of all the facts, but safe to say, the civil war that broke out in rugby league in Australia looked like making rich men of the top players in Britain. The war was being waged between two of the wealthiest media moguls the world has seen – Kerry Packer and Rupert Murdoch. Packer owned the Australian Rugby League (ARL) and Murdoch had the Super League. Murdoch's News Corp offered the British League £87 million for a five-year deal to run a summer Super League on this side of the world. At the time, it was pandemonium. Everybody was being courted, contracts were being bandied about to the top British players, money was flying around here, there and everywhere. Money like this had never been in the game before. To the players, it was like a gold rush. I was invited to meet an agent in an office in Bradford, and the invitation was by no means exclusive to me. As I say, facts were scarce, but the rumour-mill was buzzing. With a suggestion that peace could break out between the warring giants, there came a rush to sign on. If you were not signed up, so the story went, you would not be eligible for any loyalty bonus.

I signed the contract I was offered by the ARL, committing myself to join the Australian Rugby League in 1997 after my existing contract with Wigan expired. At that time, I saw a pot of gold and thought, why shouldn't I have a share of it? It was two years down the track, but I was to get a lump sum for signing and a good wage to play the game in Australia. I reacted by going to buy a car magazine to have a look for a new car to reflect my new status. That was how I came to own a BMW convertible.

It was like winning the lottery. How do you handle that? I abused it, I know that. I was immature and there was a lot of temptation. People who win the lottery say, 'I'll never change. I'll still drive around in the same car.' What are they doing the lottery for then? To have the same old Fiesta? Why gamble if you want more but you want the same lifestyle? It's a lie.

A young man signing a big contract is placed in the same

position as a lottery winner. People don't realise what grave responsibility young players have. They are thrust into a situation where everybody expects them to be a certain way. There is a lot of pressure. Money is the answer – now what was the question?

It is a danger that most people face at some level or another. If you work in an office and get promotion, you invariably want more. You want to climb to the top. Some don't mind who they stand on to get there. Take it to the extreme. Look at very successful businessmen with loads of money; some of them are still unhappy, so they go into politics because now they want power to go with their wealth.

The backlash of the battle between the ARL and Super League was felt in the Centenary Rugby League World Cup finals that began in Britain in October 1995. As a final throw of the dice, the ARL refused to select players for Australia who had aligned themselves with the Super League. Brad Fittler, the one superstar loyal to the ARL, captained an Australian team that was perceived at home to be little more than a touring party of reserves. There was uproar because Australia had left out so many of their top players, but nevertheless, I can vouch for the fact that they managed to bring an extremely strong team. Isn't that characteristic of Australia? In all honesty, they could pick three strong teams!

The Great Britain camp saw this as a massive opportunity, a great chance for us to win the World Cup. My own life was in a state of flux as I left home to join the squad. I had just given my life to God and I was putting my relationship with Amanda together after the birth of our son Cameron on 8 September.

Phil Larder – with whom I would work later, in the England rugby union squad – coached the England team. It was the first time I had been under his command. He was fanatical about his own fitness, always working out. The squad was packed with excellent players – Kris Radlinski, Shaun Edwards (until he was injured), Gary Connolly, Martin Offiah, Andy Platt, Denis Betts, Phil Clarke and Andy Farrell. We liked our chances, we really did. Our optimism did not seem misplaced, either. In front of 41,000 people at Wembley, we defeated Australia 20–16 in our opening Group One match. Our tries came from Paul Newlove, Andy Farrell, Chris Joynt and me. I crashed past the challenge of full-back Tim Brasher to score in the corner. A photographer captured the moment – I have my mouth open, fists clenched and am quite pleased with life to say the least! The result was just the start we needed. More than ever, we were consumed by a belief that we could win the World Cup.

Our next opponents were Fiji, who had walloped South Africa with their sensational attacking flair in their first game. A crowd of over 26,000 turned out at Central Park to see us beat the Fijians 46–0. Despite the imbalance, there was something good about getting to play against a nation that we would never play but for the World Cup. I managed a couple of tries.

Tonga and Western Samoa made an impression on this stage. New Zealand squeezed past Tonga 25–24 in injury time at Warrington after trailing by 12 points with just ten minutes left on the clock.

After England knocked over South Africa 46–0, we had to face Wales in the semi-finals at Old Trafford, where the capacity was limited to 30,000 as one side of the stadium was closed due to rebuilding works. Jonathan Davies, an old team-mate in the Britain line-up, was playing for Wales. So, too, were Martin Hall, Kelvin Skerrett and Neil Cowie, my mates from Wigan. I didn't know the details of how they qualified for Wales. I did know, however, that I could expect a tough game. As you can imagine with three front-row men of their calibre, there was a lot of banter flying about beforehand.

Davies will be remembered as one of the great players to have handled a rugby ball. I don't have much personal recall of his career in union, but I know of his reputation as a player of pace and imagination. I can testify that those skills did not desert him in rugby league. He caused a lot of problems whenever I played against him. He was slim, but he survived because he had speed, a masterly sidestep and he could kick a ball with great accuracy. We knew that Wales would present us with a challenge. After all, there is a rivalry that goes back forever between Wales and England on a rugby pitch.

It seemed strange to be playing against my mates and I made sure I stayed out of a few people's way. Kelvin caught me fairly – but he made certain it was fairly hard! England won the game 25–10, with Bobby Goulding replacing the injured Edwards. This match proved to be Davies' last game in rugby league.

In the other semi-final, Australia needed extra time to beat New Zealand after they tied 20–20 at the end of eighty minutes. The Aussies won 30–20.

The final was the one everyone anticipated, and the one the marketing boys wanted when the tournament began under the cloud of the ARL–Super League war. After beating the Aussies in the group, we had no reason to be pessimistic about our chances. Our belief in ourselves was genuine, but we also understood that any Australian team that has been beaten becomes a tougher proposition next time around. We knew they would use the loss to England in the first game as motivation to defeat us in the final. I suppose there was a lot of pressure on them back in Australia. The lads who had been chosen to wear the Aussie jersey had a heavy burden because, to the majority of supporters, they were representing their country only because the ARL had outlawed those players who had signed for Super League. But we respected the Australian team we had to face as including some of the best players in the world.

The final was tight, but Andrew Johns led Australia home with a superb performance from his unaccustomed role of hooker. Johns kicked four goals as Australia won 16–8 in front of 66,540 spectators. Losing 10–4 at the interval, England narrowed Australia's lead to just two points soon after the restart when Newlove scored from a powerful break from the play-the-ball on forty-four minutes. But with thirteen minutes remaining, Brasher claimed the Aussies' second try of the afternoon to ensure they were the ones celebrating at the final whistle.

HRH Prince Edward presented the trophy to Brad Fittler – and we had the worst seats in the house. Wembley is probably the worst place in the world to lose for an Englishman. As we stood there as runners-up in the World Cup, the disappointment is hard to describe. It's like a big bubble has burst and you are drowning. We were only edged out, but we had believed we could win. These were the teams:

Australia: Tim Brasher, Rod Wishart, Mark Coyne, Terry Hill, Brett Dallas, Brad Fittler, Geoff Toovey, Dean Pay, Andrew Johns, Mark Carroll, Steve Menzies, Gary Larson, Jim Dymock.

Subs: Jason Smith, Robbie O'Davis, Matthew Johns, Nik Kosef.
Tries: Wishart, Brasher
Goals: Johns 4

England: Kris Radlinski, Jason Robinson, Gary Connolly, Paul Newlove, Martin Offiah, Tony Smith, Bobbie Goulding, Karl Harrison, Lee Jackson, Andy Platt, Denis Betts, Phil Clarke, Andy Farrell. Subs: Nick Pinkney, Barrie-Jon Mather, Mick Cassidy, Chris Joynt.
Tries: Newlove
Goals: Goulding 2

It became apparent to me in the months after the World Cup that I really did not want to go to Australia, in spite of the lucrative contract that I had signed. I had rearranged the priorities in my life. I'd realised that money cannot buy happiness. I wanted my family to be happy and they wouldn't have been happy in Australia. I am convinced my relationship with Amanda would not have lasted had I gone through with the plan. I renegotiated to get out of the contract. After protracted discussions – and I could understand why the ARL was reluctant to let me go – I was released in 1997 from the commitment I had made in all sincerity at the time of signing. There would have been no mileage in keeping a discontented player. In turn, I agreed to stay with Wigan in a move that cost me financially but made me more secure in other ways.

After the big upheaval in my circumstances in 1995, the following year was to create the foundations for my future. I just didn't know it at the time. In this era, if Wigan were the champions of rugby league, Bath were the biggest club in rugby union.

The class divide as well as the rulebook meant that the two codes never met. I suppose I thought the class system was a thing of the past until I heard a union player talking about a league player as a 'peasant'. In the north, we did tend to dismiss the union players as 'rah-rahs' so we could be accused of the same bigotry.

When it was suggested that Wigan should play Bath, we thought it was someone's idea of a joke. But we soon realised it was a chance at last to show the union guys that we could play rugby. If we were figures of contempt in their eyes, we would give them something to change their minds. With a history of much rivalry and bitterness between the codes, here was the platform to display our game under a bright spotlight. The fixtures were set. In the first game, Bath would play Wigan at rugby league at Maine Road, Manchester, on 8 May. Wigan won 82–6.

The game broke down a lot of barriers and generated a torrent of respect for rugby league. Bath's Jon Callard said, 'Wigan were awesome. I had a huge amount of respect for them before the game but now they are bordering, in my eyes, on being Godlike. I would like Bath to do one rugby league training session a week. If we did that, we would be a far better side than we are at the moment.'

Paul Ackford, writing in the *Sunday Telegraph*, showered Wigan with praise:

> Wigan were light years ahead of Bath, who are light years ahead of their rugby union peers. We all knew about Tuigamala, but Jason Robinson was something else. If he ever decides to latch on to rugby union's ridiculously over-inflated gravy train, the Wigan winger could name his own price. On the evidence of this tour de force he is worth about three Ben Clarkes [Bath and England back-row forward].

Three days later, Wigan were the first rugby league side to be invited to the Middlesex Sevens, an end-of-season gala at Twickenham. Our team, with Joe Lydon in charge, was Tuigamala, Offiah, Henry Paul, Edwards, Connolly, Craig Murdoch and me.

When the ball was in open play, we scored one of the best tries I have seen. The move began in our in-goal area. I received the ball from Henry and took it up the right-hand touchline for around forty yards before handing back inside for Craig to race through to score. During the early games, there were a lot of people observing tradition by drinking in the car park. But, clearly, word reached them that something special was happening on the pitch. Curious, they steadily came into the ground. By the final, the place was packed.

We trailed Wasps 15–0 – but the reality of the scoreline was that we had never had the ball. Once we got it, the final was over. We had been determined to win, and we racked up 38 points without a reply from Wasps. 'Working class, working class, working class,' we sang jubilantly afterwards. It was funny, really, because Martin had started the song and he is anything but working class. But the point was well made, with a little northern humour. A few more barriers had been torn down and we handed a cheque for £20,000 to Wigan Schools Rugby League Association.

Stephen Jones wrote in the *Sunday Times*: 'When they [Wigan] won the ball they often took the breath away. A combination in their outside backs of Offiah, Robinson and Tuigamala would simply threaten the most serious damage to any team ever assembled in any code of rugby.'

Later in the same month, Bath defeated Wigan 44–19 under rugby union rules at Twickenham where 42,000 turned out for the match. Afterwards, Terry O'Connor – a prop for Wigan and Great Britain – was full of admiration for the Bath forwards. He said he had no idea how hard it was to play union. He was also aware that the Bath pack took it easy in the scrums for fear of inflicting damage on players with no experience of scrummaging at the same intensity.

At this time, there was a serious wind of change blowing through rugby. For example, Scott Quinnell, who had signed for Wigan in 1994 because he could make a better living in rugby league than he could as a Welsh rugby union international, was enticed to switch codes again. Richmond brought him back to union. This showed that the financial muscle of union was growing.

With rugby league changing from a winter game to a summer game, we found ourselves with five dead months from September 1996. Suddenly, there was an interest from union clubs to sign some of league's more flamboyant players. Wasps recruited Inga Tuigamala, Gary Connolly went to Harlequins while Henry Paul and I joined Bath. Martin Offiah was subject to a time-share arrangement with Bedford (rugby union) and London Broncos (rugby league).

Wigan's gates had fallen and the club was struggling for money. Removing some of us from the staff for the winter would save them paying our wages. I had been made a decent offer by Bath – if it had been rubbish money I would not have gone – but just as important as the financial rewards, I felt I had an opportunity to try something new. However, the period I spent in Bath was not without its disruptions to family life. We had not long moved into a new house in Lancashire – our first family home. We had felt the need to leave Wigan because we needed some privacy. There was a constant stream of kids knocking at the door of our house. All they wanted was an autograph, but I think there is a time and place for that. When I get home, I think I am entitled to switch off. One day I remember hearing the letterbox clink and when I went to examine what was going on, I saw two eyes peering through the gap. Then I heard a voice, 'He's in. I can see him.' It was just kids being kids, but I realised we had to get out. Wigan is a great rugby town, but we needed space and so we had to move away.

A few days later, I got in the car and went house hunting without a clue about where to look. I just drove out into the country until, down a lane, I came across a house with a For Sale board outside. An elderly woman lived in the house and she told me she used to breed Boxer dogs. The property, a traditional red-brick 1930s house, came with two acres and backed on to fields. I liked the fact that it was secluded yet only eleven miles outside Wigan. It needed work but when I brought Amanda back to view it, she took an instant liking to it, too. This house was to become our home.

But no sooner had we moved in than we moved out, if only temporarily. When I signed for Bath we rented a house in Marshfield. It was a lovely spot, but miles away from home and family. Again, it was hardest on Amanda. I was occupied by my rugby while she had to deal with a seven-month-old baby without support of family or friends. But she understood it was an opportunity I had to accept, or else regret it for the rest of my career.

I never thought I could play rugby union; I knew nothing about the game. I never even watched it. I was on a crash course, learning as I went along. I sensed a lot of people within the game were frightened of us switching successfully between the two codes. A lot of criticism came my way – with more than a little justification, I might add. I am sure people watched in disbelief. I would pick up the ball in our in-goal area and run. I didn't realise I should have touched the ball down to get a drop-out. I was trying to play a game I didn't understand. I didn't know the rules, I didn't know the strategy.

Bath's coach, Brian Ashton, was a keen fan of rugby league, and he supported me. I came to the conclusion at the time that rugby league is an easier game than union to play and watch, but then I grew up with league. I managed to keep England winger Jon Sleightholme out of the Bath team, so I can only assume I was doing something half right, even if I did want to run the ball from defence into attack. Other times I played full-back, but wherever I played I was not given to kicking.

I think Brian liked what I offered, as is confirmed in an article written by David Hands for *The Times* on 2 November 1996:

His rugby union career – all of seven weeks old – has encompassed games against sides from England, Scotland, Wales, France and, today, Italy. If variety is the spice of life, then Jason Robinson has found more in that brief time than in all his burgeoning rugby league career with Wigan. However, at 22, the world is Robinson's oyster. He joined the ranks of rugby union players with no great regard for the 'other' code, but admits that Bath have surprised him. 'It's been exciting. It's been an honour just to play for Bath against all those different teams,' he said. 'We don't have that kind of opponent in league – we may play Australia or New Zealand in Tests, so it's nice to see what other countries can produce.'

Yet if the Heineken Cup, in which Robinson plays full-back for

Bath in Treviso today, has offered him a different dimension, so has he to Bath. Brian Ashton, their coach, describes him as a unique talent; Alan Davies, who watched Robinson light the blue touch-paper under his Bristol side in their Courage Clubs championship game on Tuesday, which Bath won 76–7, is fascinated at the perceptions Robinson and his colleague, Henry Paul, bring with them. 'You have to get up on them so quickly to cut down their space, but they stand so deep and move so quickly it's not easy,' Davies admitted, ruefully. Ashton cheerfully concedes that he lost a bet he made with Robinson that, from full-back rather than his accustomed position of wing, he would be forced to kick against Bristol. 'I don't think Jason saw that as a challenge, I just don't think he recognised it as an option,' Ashton said.

'I have never seen a running style like his, but opponents underestimate his footballing brain. He reads the game so quickly and he is always willing to learn more. The other players at Bath have taken to him and the fact that he's willing to take these calculated risks has opened up their minds to all the possibilities that exist. He creates space in a totally different way, because he finds support so quickly, because he doesn't hit the line in the conventional sense but he's so swift off the mark. With that kind of talent we don't need to call moves that often and defences these days are organised against moves. If we can put the defence where we want them and use the ability we have across the width of the field, it makes defending very difficult.'

As I say, I just like to take the ball back upfield. To me, playing on the edge comes naturally. My coaches have always let me go out and play, and that is how I want it. I don't want to be put in a box and told to do certain things in certain situations. To me, the way to break teams down is by having a go, playing by instinct. I don't know I can get through the gap until one-hundredth of a second before I get through the gap. I have the confidence to believe I can beat the first man every time. That's why most times I try it. It seems others have come to accept how I play.

At the end of my period with Bath, I thought to myself, 'Well, at least I've played with the likes of Jeremy Guscott, Mike Catt and Phil de Glanville.' All of them were England players and it was an experience to be in the same team. Had I not tried the game then, I probably wouldn't have been so enthusiastic about leaving Wigan for a new life four years down the track.

10
STREET LIFE

'Sincerity makes the least man to be of more value than
the most talented hypocrite.'

CHARLES SPURGEON

She was enraged and calling me names – 'You nigger this . . .
you nigger that.' There were twenty or so people standing around
our van on a cold winter's night in Manchester and she had
gone straight for the throat. You could have cut the atmosphere
with a bread knife.

I had politely refused to give her a second hamburger – and
I knew she'd had one – until I had given out burgers to those
who had not eaten. As she screamed blue murder, cursing me,
I tried to calm her down. The old me would have jumped out
of the van and given her some well-chosen words back, but I
didn't react. I ended up apologising, in fact.

Life on the streets is easy for no one, let me tell you. For
around eighteen months I was part of a team of people who
tried to make a small contribution. We tried to be just and fair
but on the streets, as in life, there are those who abuse the
system and those who are used. In those eighteen months I
learned so much, not least about myself.

At the beginning of 1998, I was chatting with a group of friends, Rebecca, Lisa and Joshua, and we agreed that we wanted to do something of value in the community. Helping the homeless seemed like a worthwhile venture and, as there was not a problem in Wigan, we thought our services would be of most use in Manchester. We reasoned that if we took some food and clothing to where we knew homeless people chose to sleep, we would be letting them know that others cared about them.

We began by making sandwiches at home. I persuaded a nice man at Standish Self-Drive in Wigan to loan us a van and I'd collect it after training every Thursday. We had some big urns to make tea and a barbecue to cook burgers and sausages. We also made arrangements to collect clothes and blankets from those who wished to donate them to us. It was a small gesture. We knew we were not going to solve the homeless problem, but we thought we might just make a difference.

Within no time, it was apparent we were fulfilling a need. Our operation needed to be increased, so I auctioned some of my rugby kit and with the money we bought a catering unit – a mobile hamburger bar to you and me. It made cooking easier all round.

It was tiring. Sometimes we would stay around Piccadilly and Chinatown until one in the morning. After driving home to Leyland, I'd have to clear out the van and, before we had our own, have it ready to return to Wigan in the morning before going to train. Being worn out was a small price for such a rewarding experience. People would open up to us, although some had difficulty in believing that we were not being paid to turn out. I admit that I probably harboured the same prejudices towards the homeless as a lot of people. I used to walk past someone begging on the street and think, 'Why don't you get a job, mate?' But life is not that straightforward. Things that may seem easy for you and me may be really hard for someone else. One man I remember was well-educated, but he had fallen apart after his wife had left him. He just couldn't handle it.

Others had drug or drink problems and they were mixed up and felt abandoned by society. What money they had went on their addiction. We had people come to us totally off their heads; the burger we gave them was the first food they had eaten for a couple of days, or more. There were prostitutes who came to us, and they might have sustained a black eye since you saw them last. You could only imagine the desperate state of their lives, and your heart just went out to them.

These people are an underclass. They live in a world we like to shut out because it makes us afraid, uneasy and ashamed to admit that it exists. I had my eyes opened by what I saw on the streets of Manchester. After the pubs and clubs have closed, it's a dog eat dog world out there. You could tell there were certain people that everyone else feared and didn't mess with. But we tried to be friendly with everybody, and tried to share food and clothing with everyone. In the main that worked, but sometimes we would get unavoidably caught in the middle of a dispute. A fight might break out around the van; occasionally someone might go bananas like the woman who called me names because she wanted another burger out of turn. One time, someone tried to get in the van with us because someone was after him. We told him he could not stay. We could not be seen to be taking sides. We had to be seen as neutral territory where everyone was equal, where everyone could get something to eat on a freezing night when sunrise would seem an eternity away. You knew that for some of them their bed for the night was a cold pavement or a doorway and you wanted to take them home.

We were not there to judge, just to help a little. Some recognised me from rugby, and if they weren't Wigan fans they'd give me some stick. We had a few laughs. One lad I remember gave his life to the Lord and became a Christian. We had spoken and been honest with him, and I told him about my life and the things that had happened to me. He had problems of his own and we were able to relate to each other. He just needed somebody to talk with. He had run away from his problems just like I had, but he had not stopped running until he finished on the street. He decided to go along to a Fellowship meeting and the last time I saw him he was doing fine.

Those months out on the streets are probably the most rewarding I have spent; my heart was so much in it. But Amanda was heavily pregnant with our second child and I realised that I had to start spending more time at home. As much as I wanted to carry on, I understood there is a time and order to life; things are not always going to last as long as you want. We gave away the catering unit to another charity organisation that works around Manchester.

When my rugby days are over, maybe I will return to voluntary work. You never know what's around the corner, but I'd like to contribute in some way again. I can open my heart to a stranger, even if some people think of me as someone who keeps my thoughts to myself. I can share a lot of things that I have been through that I wouldn't want to shout from the rooftops. I am friendly, I think. I can get on with anyone, but my feet are still on the ground. Those homeless people in Manchester were not interested in what car I drove or the house I lived in. They were just pleased to see a group of people who showed they cared.

11
PART OF THE UNION

'I desire to do your will, O my God; your law is within
my heart.'

PSALM 40:8

Around Christmas 1999 stories began to circulate in one or
two newspapers that Clive Woodward, coach of the England
rugby union team, was interested in talking to me about
changing codes. It was purely speculative because I had not
spoken with him or anyone else from the RFU at the time.

My contract with Wigan was due to expire at the end of 2000,
and early in the year, the club asked me to discuss a new deal
with them. Perhaps they felt threatened by the stories although
there was no reason to suppose I would not stay at the club that
had been my home since I left school. That was where I stood
when I went to meet Wigan's officials. I was looking after my
own affairs at the time – after having had one bad experience,
I couldn't be bothered to search for a reputable agent to act for
me. Besides, after all these years I knew the basic principles of
negotiation and my contract was uncomplicated.

What I had not anticipated was that Wigan would offer me
less money to re-sign than the salary I was already on. I did

not know if they were trying it on with me, seeing if I would just accept their proposal without a murmur if they cited the old 'salary-cap' excuse as a reason for keeping wages down. Whatever motivated them to make the offer, I was unimpressed that the club I had played for throughout the past eight years felt they could entice me into signing a new contract by inviting me to take a pay-cut. I had already taken a cut to stay at Wigan after I rejected the chance to go to Australia on a huge contract.

I am not motivated by money, but nor am I a fool. I knew my profile at Wigan was high – and still rising – and I knew, too, that I was one of the cornerstones of the team. So why was my money going down? When I rejected their offer, they came back with a renewed deal that would give me the same as I was currently on, provided I met certain performance-related clauses. I felt I had long passed the need to prove myself to anyone at the club. Everyone knows I have always given the same level of performance regardless of any bonuses on offer.

Their next move was remarkable and, to my mind, grossly unprofessional. They tried to negotiate my contract in parallel with that of Andy Farrell as his current deal was also expiring in 2000. I was told that he would not get a penny more than me, and I wouldn't get a penny more than him. What Andy is paid is an irrelevance to me. If I had agreed to £100,000 and later found out he was on £200,000, it would not have bothered me one bit. I wanted my negotiations to be separate and private. Wigan wanted me to agree to a five-year contract, but I had no need to make a hurried decision. I told them I would get back to them.

Not long afterwards I took a phone call from David McKnight, a well-known players' agent. He wanted to talk over approaches he had received from the Rugby Football Union. There seemed no harm in accepting his invitation to meet him. As it became clear that other opportunities were being opened to me, I asked David to look after my interests because I knew he'd had experience of dealing with the RFU. Still, I never truthfully imagined leaving Wigan and my focus remained on playing well for my club.

David came back to explain the RFU had a genuine interest in me. He arranged for me to meet chief executive Francis Barron and Fran Cotton, a former prop forward for England and Sale. Naturally, this meeting took place in secret as the fewer people who knew, the less chance there was of needless speculation. Henry Paul had also been asked to meet Francis and Fran. Henry was playing for Bradford at the time and we got together at a hotel in Cheshire. The message conveyed to us was that Clive Woodward wanted to involve players from rugby league in his grand vision of creating an England team for the World Cup in Australia in 2003.

It was arranged for me to meet Clive and as soon as we had been introduced, he made it clear how much he wanted me to come over to rugby union. He stressed the opportunities that existed in the game now that it was professional and being properly structured. From a player's point of view, it is always nice to feel wanted, and Clive felt that I had some qualities he could utilise.

This was fairly radical thinking, and Clive describes the background:

I went to live in Australia for five years between 1985 and 1990. I know it's not too long ago, but rugby union and rugby league were two separate games in Britain at the time and you were severely reprimanded by the RFU if you even spoke to a rugby league player, or so it seemed. In Australia, it was fascinating to see the two games working successfully side by side. Players mixed and, without over-simplifying it, rugby union was a Saturday game and league was a Sunday game. I started to watch a lot of rugby league and developed a passion for it.

When I got the England coaching job in 1997, my immediate thoughts focused on rugby league because to me all the barriers had been taken away; both games in England were professional. When I made my comment – 'Judge me on the World Cup [1999]' – I did so because I was told I would be able to sign four or five guys from rugby league. It is the only reason I made the state-ment – which I lived to regret! With all the politics that polluted the game, the divide between clubs and country, the plan went pear-shaped. I had looked at the leading lights in rugby league – Andy Farrell, Kris Radlinski, Jason Robinson and Henry Paul. I had no doubt these guys would benefit not just England but also the sport. If they had been spread across Premiership clubs, I think it would have made a massive difference to our World Cup. But it wasn't to be because of the politics. There were so many other things going on between the clubs and the union this was just a sideshow.

I have no doubt the players were really up for this in terms of switching over, but the one player out of all of them who I could just see wanted to make a complete change in his rugby, in his lifestyle, was Jason. I don't think we ever spoke about money.

When I met Clive I was interested in what he had to say and I wanted to hear the reasons why he wanted me to consider switching to rugby union. He's right when he says I never mentioned money. I was comfortable where I was at Wigan, despite the contract wranglings. I had a testimonial due in the next year and I was established in the team and in the international team. My future was assured. I knew I could have stayed at Wigan for many years and leaving would expose me to risks I didn't need to entertain. However, I felt I had to survey my career with an open mind. Of course, I prayed for guidance. I had learned from experience in 1995 that money wasn't the answer. I didn't want to make a decision based on the wrong values. I had to make a call that was right for us all as a family. I had to assess my options properly.

I did not speak to anyone at Wigan over my contract for a while. I waited and continued to pray. One thing that was never an attractive proposition was the idea of signing for a club that would have required us to move our home. I had discovered through past experience that living in Bath was not right for us as a family. I supposed that meant, in an ideal world, staying in the region to play my rugby, whatever the code. Now there are not too many rugby union strongholds in the north west. Certainly Sale, a little club in south Manchester, hardly seemed a viable destination. For all their history, they were in more danger of folding than expanding. Then in the spring of 2000, and out of the blue as far as I knew, Sale were taken over by a massively successful businessman, Brian Kennedy. Brian takes up the story:

> About a year and a half before taking over Sale, I almost bought Hibernian, the Edinburgh-based football club I used to support. The deal fell through because they changed their mind at the eleventh hour. I was living in Cheshire at the time, so realistically it would have been difficult having a business in Edinburgh, but I had really got the bug for being involved in sport.

I had played a lot of rugby and around that time it was reported that London Scottish were in danger of going bust because they could not sustain the levels of support needed to stop the club bleeding money. I met with the RFU and presented a marketing plan to take London Scottish back to Scotland. Everybody loved the plan but it fell through on political grounds. There was already a commitment to forming district sides in Scotland and it would have been difficult to reverse that. It was shortly after that I received a call from Adrian Hadley at Sale. After hearing about my involvement with London Scottish, he felt I should consider supporting my local side, Sale.

At that point, investors in Sale had lost £8 million in three years, the club were bottom of the league, had nil infrastructure and the place was ready to go bust. There were people desperate to make a graceful exit. It was a nightmare. Club members had contemplated trying to buy back the club, but came to the conclusion they could not afford it.

For some crazy reason I went ahead and did the deal. I think a lot of it was down to the fact that I had been thwarted twice already. The risk was big, the challenge massive, but the people of Manchester had never had a professional rugby side to focus on. There were small factions at Sale, Orrell and Manchester, but they could not compete in the pond with the sharks of the game, such as Leicester, Gloucester and Bath. I took the plunge into the pond with Sale, having made sure the debt was written off. I would rather inherit a business with a lot of debt that is making money, than one without debt that is losing money. The big issue here was that the business was losing £2 million a year – and that was the risk we took. It has cost us a lot of money, but we are slowly getting there.

On day one I met Jason in a wine bar in Knutsford with his agent, David McKnight. I wanted to explore bringing him to Sale from rugby league. Jason had been messed about. He had been promised a contract to move into rugby union, but nobody had yet delivered and he had just about given up on it. And then I came along, shook hands and the deal was done.

I knew if we were going to do something here we had to make some statements. We had to get some top-class players and start winning some games. As well as building the marketing and managing and coaching infrastructure, we needed some stars on the pitch, and Jason was a world star in rugby league.

The RFU were willing to do a deal on his salary although the specifics hadn't been sorted out when we shook hands. I promised Jason I'd pay his wages, irrespective of what came from the RFU. They agreed to pay roughly 50 per cent but when it came out there was an outcry from the clubs. They threatened to boycott all matches with Sale if I took that payment. Bearing in mind the delicacy of the relationship between the union and the clubs at that point, I agreed to underwrite Jason's deal. I didn't release the RFU from their commitment, but to take the heat out of the situation, I told the clubs that I would not press for payment from the RFU right away. I agreed to pay Jason's wages until such time as the position could be re-addressed. That's exactly what happened. The RFU honoured the deal in the summer of 2001.

Clive confirmed that Brian Kennedy's intervention was critical. He, too, had been determined that the deal with Sale should not fall through. He says:

I thought about everything, even mortgaging the house. You've got to take risks in business. Running my own business – a computer-leasing company – was the best pre-requisite for this job because if you have your own business you re-mortgage your house more times than you care to think of. I was going to do it because I had made commitments to Jason and I wasn't going to let him down.

I had no doubts about the wisdom of what I was doing. Very few shared my vision. Obviously Brian did, which was important, so did Fran Cotton and Francis Barron at the RFU. Most of the press didn't really, but I was convinced I was right. I didn't think it was an especially bold move, just common sense. That's why I brought Jason into the first England training session as soon as he'd gone to Sale.

While I was deliberating my future, I had no contact with Wigan's board, yet it was continually being reported in the papers that they were getting closer to re-signing me. I didn't feel any need to chase them, and the club were not used to that. Later, I heard that other players who were trying to negotiate new deals were told they had to wait until the club knew what was happening with me. Wigan ultimately offered me a much-improved contract. Had they done so in the first place, I have no doubt that I would have stayed with them. I was extremely comfortable at the club and with my life.

But the timing of meeting Brian proved to be perfect. When he asked to meet at a wine bar, my first thought was, 'I don't go in bars,' but we arranged the appointment for teatime and had something to eat. I got on with Brian straightaway; he certainly seemed a larger-than-life character. It was also apparent he was successful in business. After I met with him, I knew I was going to make the switch. I think what most appealed was a fresh challenge. At Wigan, I was with a club that had so much history and had been so successful. At Sale, I'd be beginning again, starting a new game at the bottom.

I can understand why people had reservations about my

decision. Consider the facts: I was turning my back on a good-sized stadium at Wigan to go to Heywood Road, Sale's little ground in the suburbs, where on a good day 2,500 might come to watch the game. I was quitting a game I had played since I was a child for a game that I didn't understand – and that's the rules, never mind the playing strategies.

Many people, except those closest to me, thought I was making the move for money, but the truth is I wanted to be confronted with a new challenge. Also, I thought it was a chance to spread the word. In rugby league, everyone knew where I stood – fans, players and media. With the chance to play rugby union, I thought a door was opening to a larger world, and my story could be shared on a much bigger scale. In fact, I was able to use the media to do that from day one. Everyone was interested in my story although I don't try to force my faith. Let's face it, if something is forced on you, a natural response is to reject it; and that is especially true when male pride is involved. But if you see something works, it has a bigger impact and it is better by far for people to ask questions if they wish rather than have someone else's beliefs rammed down their throats. If someone shows interest, great, the door is open.

Before the news of my leaving Wigan was made public, Sale Sharks' media manager Dave Swanton got in touch. He lives just four miles from me, and he brought round photographs and information on the players, so I would know who everyone was when I arrived, and also videos of several games.

I had first met Swanny when he came to Wigan as media manager in March 1998. He recalls our first meeting:

I met Jason the second day I was in the building as I was doing some media training for the players. I knew he was a born-again Christian and I thought I'd better let him do the running, but I realised within about thirty seconds that he had a wonderful sense of humour. He started taking the mickey immediately and that put me at ease. When I got to Wigan, I inherited a desk diary that was three years out of date, a broken chair and a pile of correspondence that was Jason's fan mail. I think from that moment I became his personal secretary.

Swanny left Wigan to work for Peter Deakin at Warrington at the end of 1999. Peter, who sadly died early in 2003, was friendly with Brian Kennedy and earmarked for Sale. Peter had no problem persuading Swanny to join him at Heywood Road in July 2000. I laughed down the phone when Swanny called to tell me he was moving to Sale. 'And you thought you'd got away from me,' I said. He is a good friend; I think we are quite good for each other. Quite apart from his work as a media manager, he is a broadcaster, DJ and one-time bit-part actor.

Swanny understood my desire to fast-track my arrival in rugby union even as I finished out my days with Wigan. I'd seen Inga and Frano Botica having to learn rugby league when they arrived from rugby union, and I wanted to hit the ground running at Sale. I wanted to make an impact. Attention to detail was important, which is why I was pleased to have the information about the players and video film of games. I did my homework.

But before I could fully concentrate on Sale, I still had a Grand Final to play for Wigan at Old Trafford. I had already played my last home game for the club and that brought a lump to my throat. That was a sad, sad day. Astonishingly, I ended my time at Wigan as I had begun, playing against Hull. I had not formally announced I was leaving, but by then I don't think there was much doubt that this was the end for me. At the hooter, Andy Farrell and Denis Betts hoisted me on to their shoulders and paraded me around the ground. I confess to feeling unusually emotional. I appreciated in that moment that I would never play there again. As I was carried round the pitch, I had flashbacks of so many memories playing for this club, for these supporters. For over nine years, Wigan had been my life, nine magical, marvellous years. They started with wild days that degenerated into wilder nights, but over those years I mellowed and moved forward. My spiritual perception of life was formulated and moulded. I will never, ever forget the Wigan years.

And so it came to my last-ever game for Wigan – the Grand Final on 14 October 2000 at Manchester United's fabulous stadium, appropriately against our arch rivals St Helens. It would have been the perfect ending to leave the club victorious to the last, but sometimes it is impossible to have total control of the script. Besides, if sport were predictable, it would lose much of its appeal. I'd had more than my share of winning, so when we lost to St Helens there was not that same deep sense of disappointment that I had experienced on other occasions.

My old friend Apollo Perelini played for St Helens in the match, and he shortly became a team-mate at Sale.

Once we trooped back into the changing room, tired and defeated, there was a little ceremony to mark my departure. The record will show that during my years at Wigan I won the following honours: World Club Championship medal; two Challenge Cup final winners medals; four championship medals; four Premiership medals; three John Player Trophy medals; one Lancashire Cup medal; one JJB Grand Final medal. I won twelve Great Britain caps (eight tries) and seven England caps (five tries). I started 273 games for Wigan (plus eight as substitute) and scored 171 tries and one dropped goal (against St Helens in 1996).

That evening at Old Trafford, I was presented with an engraved carriage clock to commemorate my services to the club. But there was a bit of a funny atmosphere because other players were leaving the club, too, including Tony Smith and Danny Moore, and they never received a parting gift. After showering, we took the coach back to Wigan, but there had not been any arrangements made for a reception for the team. Most of the boys planned to go to a local nightclub for a big farewell celebration, but my clubbing days had ended long ago.

As the boys went their way, I walked to the car park to meet Amanda, who had been to the game. Suddenly, we were the only ones left. My mates had disappeared, not just for the night but, most of them, forever. I started the engine of the car, eased into gear and drove away from Wigan rugby club for the last time as a member of the staff. It was a strange way to say goodbye.

Three days later, I drove down Heywood Road, Sale, to start my career in rugby union. From the beginning, I felt a lot of weight on my shoulders. Those raised on rugby league called the game kick and clap. I put that down to ignorance now. I think a mutual respect exists between the players from league and union, but throughout history there has been a division between the administrators. They fought each other for years, after all. As for supporters, it is unlikely that a Wigan fan – or a fan of any rugby league club – will ever fully appreciate rugby union; and the same logic applies to those brought up on union. To most of them, league will always be a different brand of rugby.

Unsurprisingly, my move caused some people to curse me and others to acclaim me. I knew I would face a lot of criticism. I was caught in the middle of a row that started one hundred years ago. I was accused of being a traitor. Some league fans thought I had sold out for one reason – money. I received some rude letters and faced some verbal abuse. I was called a 'disgrace'. But those people were a minority. To be truthful, I understood their bitterness. I feel that in their anger and their disappointment they were confirming their affection for me as a player. They felt their team was going to be poorer for my departure and the abuse was their way of expressing that. Had I been considered rubbish, there would not have been the same response. Mostly, I felt I left Wigan with the fans' blessing. I think they recognised I had invested much time and effort in the club. Sure, I had made a good living, but I had contributed to many successful years. I really enjoyed my time at the club, but I knew that it was time for me to move on.

In doing so, I understood that I had put myself on the line like never before. If some rugby league fans wanted me to succeed as a statement of the greatness of their game, there were inevitably going to be those in union who wanted me to fail. For years, they had been arguing that union was a better game with better rugby players. The size of the media brigade that turned up for the press conference to introduce me at Sale was an indication of the interest my signing had created. I had never been confronted with a crowd of reporters or television cameras of this magnitude before. As I tried to absorb this fascination in me, it registered that no matter how high my profile had been in rugby league, it was about to be enlarged on a scale I could never have envisaged.

I knew that not everyone was rejoicing at my move. I sensed there were those hoping that I would come to Sale and play the big I am from rugby league. I was determined not to fall into that trap. My stance was uncomplicated. I declared from day one that I was the new boy, here to learn. I admitted I didn't know all the rules, but I was studying them and would get to grips with them as fast as humanly possible. I had to grow accustomed to being part of a new team, I had to get to know a new squad of players and a new play-book. I hoped my humility would strike a chord. I was also able to make it clear to a new, far broader audience about how the Lord had turned things round for me. I was here because of what He had done, and no other reason.

I made my debut for Sale against Coventry in the Tetley's Bitter Cup on 5 November and thankfully, scored a try in the closing minutes.

I was fortunate that while I had to make a lot of new acquaintances I was not entirely without friends at Sale. Apart from Swanny, there was another member of the staff at the Sharks whom I knew very well – conditioning and fitness coach Marty Hulme from Australia. When John Monie came back to Wigan for his second spell as coach, he brought Marty with him from Auckland. A decent man, Marty really understands his business and at Sale he also manages the club's academy. I recommended him to Brian Kennedy when he said he wanted to piece together a coaching team to move the club forward.

Marty had never worked in England before he arrived at Wigan in 1998, and the weather laid on a typical welcome, as he recalls:

I took my first training session on this horrible, horrible wintry morning. I was not ready for seeing players in balaclavas and gloves. I ordered them to take them off. But halfway through the session it was so cold that my whistle stuck to my lips; I was frozen. Sheepishly, I told the players they could put on their balaclavas and I said, 'For God's sake, someone give me a pair of gloves!' During that session, the boys were playing some touch football. All I can remember is this sound, swissssh. What was that? It was this slight guy hitting the ball at pace and going through about four or five other guys. I turned round to John Monie and he was laughing. I said, 'Who is that?' John told me it was Jason Robinson.

It transpired that while Marty may have been impressed with my acceleration and change of direction, not much else satisfied him. He determined to alter my training programme. Marty again:

When I first came to Wigan, I did a lot of testing on the players; it was a way for me to identify and classify them. For instance, I was astounded when I asked the boys to do a standing long jump and Jason's jump measured 3.17 metres. In ten years, I had never seen anyone jump more than 2.99 metres – that was Australia's rugby union full-back Matt Burke. I asked Jason to jump again because I was convinced I must have made a mistake in my measurement. Bang, he repeated an almost identical jump. But the thing was, he was not very fit at all. His aerobic and anaerobic base was quite poor. In games, he'd make a run and be out of breath. But he was so explosive on the pitch, he would beat his first and second man more times than not. Due to that, he had a high work rate.

When he got started at Wigan, Marty required me to do a lot of shuttle runs. He pushed me hard against the clock. He built up my base levels and I felt the improvement. But Marty's greatest asset is that he recognises that players are different individuals with different requirements. He was the first to establish a programme designed specifically for me. When he arrived, everyone at Wigan was on a blanket programme in the weight room. The more I worked on Olympic lifting, the more I blew up like Arnold Schwarzenegger. I had a sore back, I couldn't do certain lifts and I was starting to get problems. Marty and I worked together and came up with a pretty good individual programme. Now I don't do any Olympic lifting but I do a lot of work on shoulder rotation, a lot of dumb-bell power cleaning, hand cleaning and plyometrics.

I'd have to be careful with sprint training on the tartan track, too, because I'd get problems with my hamstrings and lower back. Grass was the only surface that suited me. I'm very inflexible, but Marty says that has probably helped me. It may be the reason everything holds together, an interesting theory. This is how he puts it:

I think a lot of this is his genetic make-up, but I call him a greyhound; like a greyhound he has to be handled carefully, very delicately. The slightest difference in his programme could tweak anything in Jason. I've worked with hundreds of international players from Australia, New Zealand, England and Scotland, and I have never seen anyone with his genetic make-up. When I started working with him, I suspected that other players thought I was letting him off when he was excused some of the weight programme. I had to stand up one day and explain myself, telling the boys, 'Look, you are all different and that's the way I will manage you.' I didn't single out Jason but they all knew who I was talking about.

I will not forget the day he said he was leaving Wigan. I told him, 'You can't leave this place,' and he said to me right then,

'Marty, I want you to come with me.' I was taken back by the suggestion. I was a bit up in the air about Wigan myself. John Monie had got the sack, a couple of chairmen had gone. There was a lot of instability, but I had the utmost respect for the players. I knew, too, from speaking to a number of them they respected Jason's decision even if they were saddened to lose a world-class player from their team. I spoke with my wife that night about what Jason had said.

I could see in his eyes that he was passionate about succeeding in rugby union. He was ready for another challenge. Jason and I spoke about the physical side of union – I'd spent ten years as physical education master at St Joseph's College in Sydney, one of the leading rugby union schools in the country – and I told him he would cope without a worry. More crucial was the technical side. What position would he play? I never thought he would be best suited to playing on the wing in union. You have to get the ball in his hands as often as possible – he's the best running back in the game.

He has the ability – and I don't know how he does it – but he moves in the air and can step off his left or right foot. He takes very short strides and is explosive. I'd say from a standing start over five metres, pretty much no one can touch him. I laugh at people who say he is too small. He has an amazing vertical jump.

What people outside the game don't know is that Jason has a great sense of humour. When John Monie went back to Wigan, he could tell that discipline at the club was not at the same high level as it had been when he left. We decided to get the boys back into the habit of doing a recovery session after games by going swimming. First time, I booked a pool at Wigan and they all turned up except Jason. I couldn't see him anywhere. 'Where's Jason?' I asked. I was told he was getting changed, so I gave the guys permission to start doing some laps of the pool.

I was watching them when suddenly I was aware of this guy walking towards the pool wearing snorkel, flippers, goggles and a lifejacket. It was Jason. The boys were all laughing when Jason confessed, 'I can't swim.' As he edged into the water, I had tears running down my cheeks.

Another time I had the boys playing water polo – so Jason turned up with a lilo and volunteered to be a goalie. He just laid out on the lilo.

But when we took the Sale squad to Lanzarote for warm-weather training, Jason was there in the pool at 6.45 every morning doing his laps. He had learned to swim. He swam breaststroke and finished a long time after the others, but he was determined to finish. I was tickled pink. Probably not too many people know how scared of water he is – that was a big effort and you have to respect the guy.

The truth is I have always swum like a brick. When I was young, I used to hate it when anyone dunked me. I really panicked. With all those big forwards in the rugby teams, there was always someone messing around. They'd put you under without a second thought. I needed all the help I could get; hence, the flippers and lilo. In a game of water polo, the only way I could move quickly through the water when the shots came in was to paddle the lilo. I simply have no confidence in water. I just don't float. Don't they say something about black guys' bone density being against them ever making first-class swimmers? You don't see too many medallists in the Olympic pool from Africa or the Caribbean, do you? More like Eric the Eel, the comical swimmer who competed in the Sydney Games.

Marty's version of events in Lanzarote is flattering, to say the least. Apart from being half asleep at 7 a.m., I was also freezing cold as a strong wind blew each day at that hour. I did

the first length of the fifty-metre pool in about ten minutes –
a personal best! To get back to the other end I had to do about
four different strokes. I was shattered. I felt light headed and
sick; and that was supposed to be the warm-up. I was cold and
I had earache. I just wasn't meant to swim. Funny thing was
that each day when they opened the gates to the pool, Apollo
Perelini and Bryan Redpath would come out. They'd say,
'Thanks lads, we've done ours.' Apparently, they had climbed
the gates to make an early start. But I was suspicious of them
from the beginning. I knew Apollo liked the water about as
much as I did. He couldn't have knocked out more than two
lengths – but I cottoned on to their little scam too late.

All told, though, my transition from Wigan to Sale was positive from whichever angle you look at it. Everyone at the club
wanted to assist me on my journey through a sharp learning
curve. Management and supporters all got behind me and I
felt comfortably accepted in a short time.

Home games were switched to Friday evenings for the
2002–03 season, in order to avoid clashing with Saturday afternoon football at old Trafford and Maine Road, and we sold out
most of them, with crowds of around 5,500, but in order to
generate enough cash, we need to get the crowds up to mini-
mally 10,000. That means we have to move from Heywood
Road, and for the 2003–04 season, we will have a new home
at Stockport. There is a high degree of professionalism
throughout the club, and no alcohol culture. The guys can party
with the rest of them, but there are no big boozers.

Brian encourages an athletic culture, led by head coach Jim
Mallinder and rugby manager Steve Diamond – and Marty
hates the players drinking. Brian says he doesn't allow a boozy

culture in any of his businesses, which range from manufac-
turing to retailing kitchens and double glazing, with an accu-
mulative turnover of about £300 million. His strength, he says,
is getting in the top people, and the same formula is applicable
to sport. He describes his management style like this:

When I came to Sale the playing side was terrible; there were a
few good players but not many. The one thing I detested about it
was the politics on the playing side. The politics among coaches,
players and players' wives was all so much rubbish. I quickly cleaned
it out because it destroys morale and teamwork, and diminishes
focus. I just will not allow it. I meet with the management a
minimum of once a week and we go through everything in detail
with a view to keeping the relationship clean, clear and friendly.

I go to every game and I'm frantically nervous. I'm over-excitable.
I take defeat too personally and I enjoy victory too vigorously, so
I'm probably a lot more emotive than I should be; but that's my
make-up. Once I walked out of a game at Gloucester because we
completely capitulated. We were complacent. We were quiet. We were
not passionate and without that you cannot perform. I just couldn't
watch it any more – and I'd do exactly the same again.

I want this club to operate as a business that does not require
me to lump in a million quid a year forever more. The second
priority is to become winners and the two ambitions are inextri-
cably linked. Are players overpaid? I think some of the overseas
prima donnas are, but in general I don't think so.

When we signed Jason I think it was a good day for us and a
great day for the wee man! But there is no one single face in this
business or in this club. We are all part of a team. He is an important member of the squad, but this is not a one-man show, and
Jason does not behave like it is. Truthfully, he gets embarrassed by
the publicity.

Perhaps it is easier now to understand why I so readily bought into the vision of Brian Kennedy. One fundamental difference between rugby league and rugby union that I had anticipated, however, was the profile notes on players in newspapers and programmes. In union, they will write, 'So and so was educated at such and such a school, went to this university and achieved these academic honours.' At first, my pride was hurt. I have no qualifications and this was letting me know, and everyone else besides. It touched a nerve, all right.

After a while I realised that's me. While Mark Cueto at Sale, for instance, can boast a BSc (Hons) I laughingly say I have an N.O.N.E. I didn't do well at school and that is a regret. I do wish I had tried harder, but I think I have shown people that it is possible to make something of your life no matter where you start out from.

In modern times, Sale may have fallen a long way behind Leicester, Bath and Newcastle, but in Brian they have a chairman who is interested in the future not the past. That is all it took to persuade me to jettison rugby league and join the rah-rahs! There is an adventurous rhythm to the game these days. It can no longer be ridiculed as kick and clap.

12
HUNTING WITH THE LIONS

'But seek first his kingdom and his righteousness, and all
these things will be given to you as well.'

MATTHEW 6:33

The day I learned I was to be a Lion I started off more
concerned with trying to keep my Great Dane, Samson on the
premises than playing rugby. He is the Harry Houdini of the
canine world.

Not having made the preliminary touring party of sixty-seven
players – and that was of little surprise since I had been playing
rugby union with Sale for just a matter of months – I never
thought for a second that I would be included in the British
and Irish Lions squad to tour Australia in the summer of 2001.
Although I had been fast-tracked into the England squad, I had
yet to start a game for my country. So on the morning of 25
April, the day the Lions party was being announced in front of
a large media assembly at Heathrow's Crowne Plaza Hotel, I
was fixing a fence in our garden. I am no great shakes as a
handyman, more a labourer than anything else, but I had to

try to find a way of preventing Samson from escaping from the area of the garden that we had designated for him. I had repaired the fence before only to find him in the front garden a few hours later. For the size of him, I could not imagine how he managed it, so I decided to spy on him to see where he was getting out. He was unfussy in his choice of escape routes. He could go under the chainlink fence, despite the fact that it practically reached the ground. He just wriggled his body lower and lower until he was out. Another time, I saw him lean on the fence and because he was so tall, he'd flip himself over the top. This dog had to be kidding me.

I was engaged in attempting to Samson-proof the fence when my mobile rang. It was a journalist asking how I felt about being chosen for the Lions. That was the first indication that I would be going, but I had to tell him that I had no comment to make as I had heard nothing to confirm his information. The next call was from Dave Swanton. He had heard the news from Peter Jackson of the *Daily Mail*, who warned him there would be a lot of media interest in my selection. The conversation went on these lines:

Me: 'Hello, Dave. What's up?'

Swanny: 'You got the call. You're going on the Lions tour.'

Me: 'Oh, right, fine. I'll just go and finish what I'm doing to my fence.'

I may appear to take everything in my stride, but in fact I was delighted and shocked in roughly equal measure. At the time, our television was unplugged at the mains and the aerial was disconnected. We were not happy with the programmes on offer, especially for the children, and used the television to watch carefully chosen videos. Hurriedly, I put all the wires back together. I wanted to confirm the squad on Teletext, and there was my name, all right, the wildest of wild cards.

Swanny wanted me at the club to give reaction to the media, so I headed down the motorway, realising that my life had taken another surprising shift of direction. After such a short career in rugby union, I had become one of eighteen Englishmen, ten Welshmen, six Irishmen and three Scotsmen named to tour under coach Graham Henry. Swanny reckoned I swung my selection in our game against London Irish not long before the touring party was finalised. 'That was your big game of the season,' he told me. 'There were three Lions selectors in the stand – though you weren't to know – and you took the Irish apart on your own.'

As I drove to Sale, I was trying to comprehend what being selected meant. With my patchy knowledge of rugby union history, I did not begin to appreciate the honour attached to being in that special band of men until I did some hasty research. Swanny had acquired a replica Lions jersey for me to wear at a photo shoot that afternoon and I gave a standard series of interviews. My surprise and pleasure must have been evident to all those who attended the media conference. Afterwards, I determined to get a copy of the video 'Life with the Lions', the film that recorded from the inside the previous tour, to South Africa, in 1997.

In his post-tour book, *Henry's Pride*, Graham Henry wrote that it was my unpredictability that had won me a last-minute place on the tour:

Ian McGeechan says that the success of a Lions tour is 80 per cent dependent on the selection of the squad. Our evaluation of players started as early as possible and carried on for nine months between August 2000 and the squad announcement on 25 April 2001. Although we identified a core of about 20 'very probables' pretty quickly, the exhaustive nature of the process didn't prevent some of the choices hanging in the balance right up until the last minute.

Roff, Burke, Walker and Latham [Australians] are all equally comfortable on the wing or at full-back, whereas Dafydd James, Ben Cohen and Dan Luger don't offer the same flexibility [for the Lions]. The one player who did have some experience as both a wing and a full-back was Jason Robinson, who had played in both positions for his club Sale Sharks in 2001.

This was an irony in itself, because Jason had only recently converted from rugby league and had less experience of life at the top level in union than any other wingman. But we knew he had priceless gamebreaking ability. He'd flashed it in those brief, half-hour cameos for England in the Six Nations. He was extremely quick and he fairly fizzed about the field, he had a jagged step off either foot that could ruin a defender inside a stride – there one moment and away the next, like a Gerald Davies for the new millennium. He had a compact, powerful physique, played low to the ground and was expert at spinning out of a tackle.

The knock on him was, of course, his lack of experience, especially as a defender, at the top end of the union game. Even here we had a crumb of comfort, knowing he had marked [Australian] Wendell Sailor many times during his time in rugby league, and Sailor is a man of [Jonah] Lomu-type proportions whom many believe to be the best winger in either code. Robinson was used to defending his lack of size, to large people trying to run over the top or obliterate him under the high ball pumped into the corner.

That was how I had been chosen, then. But on the day my selection was announced, most pundits speculated that I would

135

be used as an impact player brought off the bench because that's how they had seen me used by England coach Clive Woodward. I had other plans. I was determined I would make the Test team in Australia. From what I could tell, I had nothing to lose.

When I looked at the names in the squad, I recognised most of them, but putting a face to the name was an altogether more difficult prospect. Amanda has a habit of getting newspapers if she thinks I am going to be in them and the next day's papers carried pictures of the Lions and short profiles on each of us. I had a new quiz to play – name that Lion. To try to get to know who was who before meeting my fellow tourists, I spent ages poring over the photographs of them. I would then cover up the names and attempt to identify them one by one. It had worked with my team-mates at Sale, but of course, if all else failed I could use my faithful fall back plan available to all Yorkshiremen – when in doubt, call the person you are speaking with 'mate'. We do that all the time where I come from, so there is no danger of causing offence.

While I was excited at being part of the Lions, I knew I could not spend seven weeks apart from my family. The obvious solution was to take them with me. My tour fee would cover the cost of travel and accommodation for Amanda and the children, and I would arrange to meet with them at convenient times on the tour. This compromise worked even more successfully when Amanda's parents said they would like to make the trip as well. This meant that Amanda had help with Cameron and Jemimah, barely 15 months old. When Amanda's sister Melanie declared she would like to be in Australia, along with her daughter Heather, I had a guarantee of my own fan club.

Life with the Lions began in camp at Tylney Hall in Hampshire. For the first time in my life I felt the motivation to keep a diary, and I think it is possible to detect a rhythm of the great adventure, the good and the bad, by including some extracts from my scribbling here. These thoughts were written in an A4 desk diary each night. Some offer insight, particularly into the pre-tour preparation, some observations are more banal. From the beginning, the controversial workload – which, in the final analysis, was condemned from inside the Lions squad as well as by the critics – can be seen to be demanding.

Wednesday, 23 May – Not had much time to think ahead really. I have been very busy trying to put the house in order before I go away. I have got somebody to look after the dogs, and booked my flight to London. I have had calls and encouraging letters from Christians from all over the country who will keep me in their prayers.

Saturday, 26 May – It's never easy leaving home and going away for seven weeks, but thankfully I will see the family in three weeks. I could feel once again that they didn't want me to go, and it always seems harder for Cameron to accept. They waved me off as I left in the taxi, Amanda having tears in her eyes. I flew to London and met Phil Larder [coach], Ronan O'Gara [Irish stand-off] and Donal Lenihan [manager] in the airport. Thankfully I was introduced because I didn't know their names. I got a cab with Phil and on the way we were nearly in a crash. Unfortunately, the traffic came to an abrupt stop and the driver's reactions were a bit slow, causing us to skid for about twenty metres, pulling up just short of the car in front. Phil and I went a bit pale.

We arrived at the hotel in one piece and went to our rooms where we were greeted by four large kit bags. I have never had so much kit in my life! Sunglasses, watch, trainers, flip-flops, boots to keep as a memento, leather jacket . . . for about an hour I looked through the bags and tried stuff on. My room-mate was Matt Perry and I was glad. He's a nice lad and I know him from my Bath days.

We had our first [squad] meeting at 4 p.m. and for the first time I felt like a Lion. It was good to meet the rest of the players, some new and some I already know. We had head and shoulders photos taken, in our Lions shirts, and after that we were given a Sony camcorder each to keep. I couldn't believe it. We had dinner then had our first session with Impact, a team-building company. This consisted of various obstacles we had to get through in groups of ten. It was a great way to get to know the other players. We had a race at the end with the other four teams and we came second. We all made some input and felt comfortable in each other's presence.

I phoned the family and Cameron's already missing me. Tomorrow it all starts. We have two training sessions and two Impact sessions. Looking forward to getting back into business.

Sunday, 27 May – 8.20 breakfast, 9.00 team meeting with Graham Henry and Steve Black, the conditioner.

Had our first training session together and it went really well. We split into two teams and ran through some moves. At first it was a casual run through, just to get familiar, but when we linked up with the forwards it became more intense. We finished off with some kicking with Dave Alred (kicking coach) and I soon found a new kicking partner in Mark Thomas. Like me, he's not a good kicker, so we felt more comfortable working together.

After the session finished, we had another meeting with Impact. We started by playing a game like paper, scissors, rock, but this was called giants, wizards and dwarfs. We split into two teams, lined up against each other, and chose one of the three options in order to beat the other team. Then, in groups, we wrote down what we thought the character of a good Lions team should be, i.e. confident, disciplined etc. We spoke about our goals openly.

After lunch I lay on top of my bed for an hour, feeling very tired. There's a lot to get through today and it seems we have no time to ourselves but this should improve as time goes on.

For the afternoon's Impact session, we were told to bring a towel and a change of clothes so this meant it involved water. I'm not a great swimmer so anything involving water doesn't go down well. Anyway, we headed off to an unknown destination, eventually arriving at a water park to be told we were dragon-boat racing. After practice, we got ready for the first race. My team came second. We were doing well until the last hundred metres when our technique went to pieces. In the next race we were better, and won. I had a sore back after that, and I don't think I'll give up rugby to race dragon boats!

Later, we had our second rugby session of the day, which involved rucking technique and going through our new plays, finishing with some kicking drills. I stayed out with the goal kickers to do some extra, and got back to my room at 8 p.m. I tried on some of our casual wear to find my trousers were about two feet too long. Hopefully, they will be altered before we set off for Oz. I watched a video on Australia before going to bed very tired. Tomorrow will be the same – 9 a.m. to 9 p.m.

Monday, 28 May – Didn't want to get up this morning because I feel shattered. The team meeting was followed by training. We went through more moves and set-plays from lineouts, followed by some kicking. After training we had another Impact session. I wasn't looking forward to it because I was tired, but once we found out what we were doing things were different. We split into four groups of about twelve, and were given several different instruments. We had to get the rhythm right and create a tune. This was an enjoyable activity and everyone joined in 100 per cent. After getting our tunes right, we had to join up with the others and play as one. I was playing the drums and my arms were killing me.

After lunch we went training in Aldershot. It was quite a good session on a hot bank holiday. At dinner, I could see the effects of the sun on most of the players. I think there will be more suncream applied tomorrow.

At 7.30 we had our fifth Impact session, which involved writing down personal things about ourselves. This was hard in a way because we then had to stand in front of the others and explain what we had written down, although it was good to find out a bit more about the other players. I said a bit about my personal life, and I think what I said was honest and from the heart. I thought it might affect some of the other players, but even if it didn't affect anyone, at least they know where I stand. Time to go to bed.

Tuesday, 29 May – No training sessions, but still a busy day. After breakfast we had our sixth Impact session. We split into groups and had to achieve various tasks, involving for some overcoming the fear of heights. One task was to climb a very tall post and stand on a two-feet-square board at the top. That seemed fine, but we had to try to get four people on the top together. We started with Donal Lenihan, who wasn't keen on heights. He got to the top and the next man followed. Once he was up, we realised we had a problem – Donal's feet were taking up nearly the whole platform so there was limited space for everyone else's feet. After a lot of shuffling around, we managed to get four people on the tiny platform. It seemed everyone enjoyed the challenge.

There was a press conference in the afternoon, and I did quite a lot of interviews. We had the team photo and I was stood at the back next to Austin Healey. We seemed to be the smallest, so we stood on pillows to increase our height.

This evening we had the sponsors' dinner at Planet 2000 in London. Zinzan Brooke and Gavin Hastings were guests and they wished me all the best. Arrived back at 12.20 p.m. very tired.

Wednesday, 30 May – Training at Aldershot once again and the weather was very warm. It's the third day on the trot that it's been hot and everyone's covered in suncream. We had a good session covering lineouts, defence, kick-offs and kicking. We seem to be improving but we realise there's a long way to go.

During the tour, I will be doing some work with a paper called *London Metro* and Teletext, and there may be something with the *Daily Mail* when I get back. I have just okayed *The Beano* article, so a few things are starting to happen.

We had our seventh Impact session during which we discussed our code of conduct for the tour. We talked about discipline, supporting each other whether playing or not, dress and many more topics. The session took over three hours, but it was important to get these things sorted out before we fly to Australia.

After dinner most people went out for a pint so I sorted out my bags and went for a swim. I arranged to meet Steve Black the conditioner but he never turned up. This must be down to one of two reasons. First, he has been bitten that much that his legs have swollen and he is taking antibiotics; or when I thought he said he was going to the pool, he has such a strong Geordie accent he could have been saying he was playing pool. Anyway, I'll ask him tomorrow what happened to him.

Thursday, 31 May – Our last training session before we leave. It went quite well. I went into Basingstoke to get a few things. I also had my tour cheque to bank so as not to lose it!

After dinner I tried once again to sort out my bags. I've got that much stuff that I'll have to leave a suitcase and a large box behind. I was all packed and ready to go by 11.15 p.m. I feel a lot more comfortable with all the boys. Hopefully, we can take all this with us and continue to build both on and off the pitch.

Friday, 1 June – Arrived at Heathrow and were greeted by the media and some supporters. We are travelling business class, which is great because normally in league we would fly economy. On the first leg of the flight I took a sleeping tablet and managed to get five hours in. On the second leg we were told to try to stay awake to compensate for the time difference.

Saturday, 2 June – We arrived in Perth and, going through customs, a few of the lads got stopped because they were carrying protein supplements in tubs. This seemed strange, but they took one tub off them and let them keep the other!

I have never been to Perth before so I am quite excited. We are staying in Fremantle, which is like stepping back in time. I didn't expect to see old houses and buildings. It's a bit like 'Little House on the Prairie'. My roomy is Dafydd James. He's a nice lad and easy to get along with.

We dropped our bags and got ready for a light training session one hour after arriving. This took place at an Aussie Rules club (Fremantle) just up the road. We will use the facilities over the next week. Had dinner and went up the road to a games arcade with a few lads. Competed on car games and shooting before having a hot chocolate and heading to bed extremely tired. Have to be up at 6.50 a.m. tomorrow.

Sunday, 3 June – Had our first training session at about 8 a.m. It was throwing it down, which wasn't expected, but it woke us up if nothing else. Training seems to be getting better every day and the team spirit is growing quickly. We got back from training later than expected so they cancelled the midday session. We were pleased with this call as the boys were very tired.

Our next session was open to the public. It's the most people I have ever seen watching training. The intensity was quite high and we look a lot sharper. About one hour after that session I went to do some weights at the gym with a few of the boys. When I got back, I rang Amanda. It was great to speak to her and Cameron and I realised just how much I miss them. I can't wait to see her on 12 June. As they say, absence makes the heart grow fonder. Well, time to go to bed again.

Monday, 4 June – Training 10 a.m. I have never been as stiff as I feel now. Most, if not all, the players are the same, so it was hard to get warmed up this morning. During training I went over on my ankle, but thankfully it was only a strain. I missed the afternoon session because of it, but I don't think the rest will do me any harm.

Tuesday, 5 June – Woke up around 5.15 a.m., prayed, and went down for an early breakfast, armed with my Bible. I had a good read, and realised that there are many things to work on. I need more knowledge of the word and its meaning.

The team playing on Friday trained a bit earlier than the team playing on Tuesday in Townsville, which includes me. We had our first afternoon off. I went into Perth with a few of the boys. We had made all of fifty yards when we had a food stop at McDonald's.

Later in the evening, all the boys went out for a meal. It was good to get out of the hotel and relax. There was enough to feed the whole of Preston. By the time we had finished eating garlic bread, bruschetta, mussels and pizza, I was full. The worst thing was that this wasn't what I ordered. I still had a salad to come, followed by a pepper steak. The steak – or should I say half a cow – came with chips but I could only manage a third of it.

The papers in England have been quick to publish news of my ankle strain but thankfully there's nothing to worry about.

Wednesday, 6 June – Day off! Stayed in bed until 10 a.m. There were a few things organised including golf, shooting and fishing, but I chose to visit Perth. I am determined to see as much of Australia as I can to go with the rugby fields and hotels. I got a taxi to Kings Park, set high above the river and overlooking the city. The views were amazing, and I filmed it with my camcorder. It is a great spot for walking and playing around with the family. I walked into the city and had a good look around. I bought a shirt in a shop owned by a lad from Warrington. He recognised me and we had a little chat. After a few hours I returned to the hotel and chilled with the boys.

Thursday, 7 June – Players 1 to 22 are preparing for their game, so we will be training in the afternoon. I had an easy morning, then lunch with Jammo [Dafydd James]. I am finding it very hard to get warmed up prior to training. My feet and groin are sore and my body very stiff. Most people feel the same way. We had a good session and went back to base. I did some extra work with Steve Black on the boxing. I'm not used to doing boxing, and it took quite a bit out of me. I took my tired body to the jacuzzi to relax and almost fell asleep. I had a massage before I rang Amanda and the kids. Went to bed and had quite a poor sleep.

Phil Greening got injured in training and looks quite bad. Find out tomorrow how he is.

Friday, 8 June – Game day v. Western Australia. We had a training session this morning with a few missing due to injury. It was good despite only twelve taking part. It seems people are picking up a lot of knocks in training.

We left the hotel at 4.30 p.m. heading for the WACA Stadium. This was our first game, and the boys wanted to set the standard. They seemed ready for this one as they took the field, and it didn't take long before we scored a try, and then the floodgates opened. Western Australia were very poor, going down 116–10, but it was a good start for us. Scott Quinnell got man of the match with a good performance. We left thirty minutes after the game as the players who are playing on Tuesday have training at 7 a.m.

Saturday, 9 June – Woke up at 6.30 a.m. for the early training session. We worked on basic structure from lineouts, scrums and some attack and defence. We left for Townsville at 10 and a private charter plane was waiting for us at the airport. At 11.30, it started to throw it down and the clouds were black. When it rains over here it certainly rains! We were a bit concerned to say the least. I prayed that the weather would ease before we left at 12, which it did, but there were more problems. The navigation system on the plane wasn't working. At 2.30 they informed us we couldn't go on this plane. They had another one on standby, but there was something wrong with that one as well. They were 80 per cent sure the problem would be resolved. Our new flight time was 5.30 p.m. so rather than stay in the airport, we left for the nearest hotel, had something to eat and chilled for a while. We caught our flight and got into Townsville at 2 a.m. My new room-mate is Matt Dawson, who is a nice lad. I didn't get to sleep until 3.30 a.m.

Sunday, 10 June – Morning off, team meeting at 12. During the meeting we went through a couple of things that were good and a few of the things we need to improve. We had the afternoon off, but I felt a bit tired and stiff, probably due to the travelling and hanging around yesterday, so I went to the gym with a few of the boys to get the cobwebs out.

Later, we watched the second State of Origin series (Queensland v. NSW at rugby league). The game wasn't as good as I thought it would be, but I'm sure it will be a great third and last game.

Monday, 11 June – Players 1 to 22 trained at 10 a.m. This was our final session before the game tomorrow, so we had to make sure things are right. It's been a hot day and the sweat was pumping out of everyone. We will have to get used to the heat as it will be warm tomorrow night. I'm really looking forward to this game, with it being my first Lions appearance. Ben Tune has pulled out so I don't know who I'm playing against.

We had a team meeting this evening, taken by David Young. He talked about how much being a Lion meant to him and how much it should mean to us. It was an honest and good talk given by a man who has been there before. I went for a walk after that with Blackie and Jonny [Wilkinson]. We ended up by the cinema but there was nothing much on. 'Pearl Harbor' was the only thing. It had already been on for an hour, but we decided to go in anyway. Armed with popcorn, drinks and sweets, Blackie went first and, to our surprise, fell down in the aisle. He got up and sat down. Jonny and I were in stitches. Within five minutes Blackie fell asleep. How he could remember what happened baffles me. I'm sure he's seen it before. Afterwards, we headed back to the hotel, having enjoyed a good laugh together.

Tuesday, 12 June – Queensland President's XV at the Dairy Farmers' Stadium, Townsville. We met in the morning just to have a chat and a walk through. It was a very hot day so we stayed out for twenty minutes only.

The rest of the day was ours, so I went for a stroll up the beach, stopped at a café and had lunch overlooking the sea. It's a different way of life over here. There doesn't seem as much hustle and bustle.

I'm trying to relax as much as possible so as not to waste nervous energy.

We met at 5.15 p.m. and I was quite nervous – my first game for the Lions and my first game for two months. The first half didn't go so great, with the team not playing to our potential. We never had good field position, turned over too much ball and played as individuals. A few penalties were awarded against me for holding on to the ball in the tackle. I also got dumped midway through the first half and lost the ball as well.

The second half was totally opposite to the first. We scored within seconds of the whistle. We started to draw their defence into the middle, which left space out wide. I got one try, then another, then another and before I knew it I had scored five tries. This will be a day I will never forget. Five tries on my Lions debut! But I'm not going to get carried away – we have much tougher games ahead. But what a start! I can't wait to see Amanda and the children tomorrow. Half-time Lions 10–6, full-time Lions 83–6.

Wednesday, 13 June – Woke up this morning thinking we would be doing some rehab, but instead we were involved in a full session. This didn't go down very well with most people who played last night. We were very stiff and it's hard to get motivated for a full session in those circumstances. I think we are now realising this is how it is going to be on this tour. We finished the session about two hours later. Then we had to eat, do a pool session and get ready to do some interviews within half an hour. There seems to be no time to do anything.

We flew to Brisbane in the afternoon, and after arriving at the hotel, I threw my bags in the room and went straight round to see Amanda. She's staying at the Dockside Apartments. It was great to see her and the children. I've really missed them and look forward to spending time with them over the next four days.

Thursday, 14 June – Got my training out of the way and went to fetch Cameron. We had a great morning playing table tennis and swimming. Back at the apartment, I fell asleep on the sofa. I felt shattered and couldn't move for a couple of hours.

Had to go back to the hotel for a team meeting, and after that we all went out to a local Chinese restaurant. We hadn't pre-ordered and it took ages for the food to come out. The boys began to get impatient, tapping on the table and banging knives and forks. Two hours later, full to the brim, we headed back to the hotel.

Friday, 15 June – Training in the morning. During the afternoon I went round the shops, hoping to meet Amanda who was also having a mooch. I never saw her so I headed back to the hotel. I was sitting in the lobby, making a call, when to my surprise, I saw Shaun Edwards walking towards me. He's doing some coaching with Wayne Bennett (Brisbane Broncos), and learning a lot from Wayne, but the Aussies are struggling to understand his Wigan accent. The Broncos played Paramatta tonight. I was going to go to the game, but went over to Amanda's instead. Brisbane got beat by a very strong Paramatta side.

Saturday, 16 June – Queensland Reds. We had our walk through in the botanical gardens. This was our best performance to date, with the forwards setting a good platform. I was on the bench, and by the time I came on the game had already been won. Nevertheless, it was more valuable experience. I played for the last twenty-two minutes and did what I could with the time. I had no knocks so the body is holding up well at the moment. Lions 42–8.

Sunday, 17 June – Did some rehab this morning, which consisted of ten minutes on the bike, followed by the pool and spa. I got this out of the way by ten o'clock so that I could spend some time with the family before I left for Sydney. We went to the park for a picnic and played rugby and piggy in the middle. We don't seem to get too much time back home to do things that involve all of us.

The apartment where Amanda and the children are staying isn't really clean, the dishwasher doesn't work and there is noise from the bar downstairs. These apartments used to be a hotel and the décor hasn't changed. They do need a lick of paint. I didn't want to leave for Sydney without finding them somewhere else to stay, but by the time we saw somewhere, I had only thirty minutes, so it was a bit of a rush. We took the new accommodation from Monday.

They came to my hotel to see me off and I won't see them for about ten days. We flew to Manly this evening. I have been named in the starting line-up for Tuesday's game against Australia A and I'm looking forward to the challenge. Mark Bell [former Wigan player] called and I'm looking forward to seeing him.

Monday, 18 June – I had a good night's sleep, the first in about a week. I've been sharing with Rob Henderson, known as the Snorer. He's great but it was like sleeping in a room with a real lion – actually, more like a bat. He could sleep through the day, and then at night he'd come alive. At 1 a.m. he'd want to chat. You'd be half asleep and he'd be ordering room service pizza and chips. Really funny! I'm not rooming with him again – can't handle his snoring.

We trained this morning at Manly RU club, which is 250 yards from the hotel. We dropped a few balls and it didn't go as well as it has been going. That said, the boys are ready for this game. We all want to continue our winning run and boost our chances of a Test place.

After training, I checked where Amanda will be staying so that there will be no problems when they arrive. I watched Dan Luger, Darren Morris and Brian O'Driscoll, my room-mate, try surfing. It looked a tiring experience but they seemed to be having fun. This evening's team meeting was taken by David Young.

I have started to put together my own video tape on the matches I play in, for a keepsake. I've picked out various tries, tackles etc.

I had a call from Mark Reber [former Wigan player] and am meeting him on Wednesday. I also spoke to Puma who will be sending me some more gear plus some pink roller skates for Amanda.

Tuesday, 19 June – Australia A. Another long day due to the night kick-off. We left at 2 p.m. because we had a one hour thirty minute coach trip to Gosford. We stopped at a hotel when we got there, for some food and a rest. It reminded me of Crossroads. The journey seemed to have zapped everyone and we lounged, snoozing in our chairs. We had our strapping done in the hotel due to a lack of space in the changing rooms.

This was our biggest test so far, and it turned out to be our worst performance to date. We gave away too many penalties, lost most of our kick-offs, and theirs, and also lost many lineouts. Lack of possession meant we never got many chances out wide to attack them. We also seemed to be very flat. Was this down to too much training or lack of preparation before the match, or was it just one of those days? We came back towards the end, but it was too little too late. I scored near the end, bringing my tally to six tries, but everyone was disappointed by the way we played.

Perhaps this is a blessing in disguise and will catapult us forward. The best way to respond is by coming back stronger and beating the Waratahs on Saturday. I was chosen for the random drugs test so I had to drink a lot of liquid. Thankfully, it took only thirty minutes or so to produce the goods. The last time I had to do one, it took me over two hours!

Unfortunately, Mike Catt was injured and won't play any further part in the tour. Scott Gibbs has been called in to replace him.

Playing with Sharks – the day I signed for Sale in October 2000.

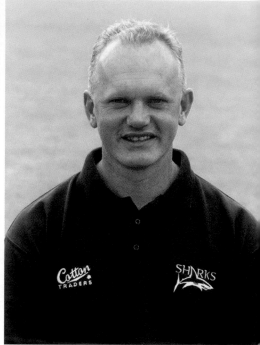

Running into a new world, I take the field at Heywood Road for my Sale debut against Coventry on 5 November 2000.

Australian fitness coach Marty Hulme and I first worked together at Wigan and I am glad he followed me to Sale.

A try in my first game for Sale provided a great start to my new life.

I am probably the only Shark with an aversion to water, as Sale fitness coach Marty Hulme, next to me, will testify.

Dave Swanton (*right*), good friend and sometime DJ, is Sale's gregarious public relations officer, assisted by his son Dan.

Jim Mallinder has done an excellent job as head coach at Sale; he also coached England on their 2003 summer tour.

Club chairman Brian Kennedy – still one of the lads at heart – shares his pleasure with captain Bryan Redpath after Sale's victory over Pontypridd in the final of the 2002 Parker Pen Shield.

After big days with Wigan, it is exciting to play a role in Sale's triumphant breakthrough in the Parker Pen Shield.

My travelling support on the Lions 2001 tour to Australia. *Left to right*: David and Lynne Whitehill, Cameron and Amanda.

Signing supporters' shirts was a breeze after an unforgettable Lions debut when I scored five tries against a President's XV at the Dairy Farmers Stadium in Townsville.

A moment to cherish for a lifetime – I evade Australian full-back Chris Latham on the outside to race in for the Lions opening try in the First Test at the Gabba, Brisbane.

The quiet before the storm – captain Martin Johnson (*left*) surveys his men immediately before the First Test.

This try for the Lions in the decisive Third Test – my tenth try in seven games – was scant consolation as we lost a really close series 2 1.

Coach Graham Henry shakes my hand at the end of the Third Test, but at that moment no words can heal the wounds inflicted by Australia's 29–23 victory.

I am blessed to have superb support from various companies. Here I am running for an advertising campaign for Marks & Spencer's 'view from' range of leisurewear.

Michael Owen scores for England in another code of football, but we both endorse Tissot watches.

Land Rover's campaign for this photo-shoot was entitled 'Built to Tackle Anything'; I am happy to say that on this occasion the camera does lie and I never met my co-star in the flesh.

Wednesday, 20 June – Arrived back late and got to sleep about 3 a.m., so I struggled to get up for the 10 a.m. meeting. We went to a local gym afterwards and did some weights followed by the spa. I've been named on the bench for Saturday's game, which meant another session at 2.30 p.m. I must admit I wasn't looking forward to it, being shattered. After about two hours it was over and I went to my room wearily.

Thursday, 21 June – Day off! They don't come very often . . . I had a relaxed morning, waking around 10 a.m. We had a game of volleyball and a bit of cricket before trying our hand in one of the lifeboats. We rowed out and tried to catch a wave to come back in. This turned out to be quite dangerous because if you get your oar caught in the water, you can't get it back out, so the oar traps you in your seat.

This evening all the team went into Sydney to a place called Doyles that overlooks the Opera House. It's a well-known seafood restaurant and most seemed to enjoy it. I'm not into seafood so the closest I came was smoked salmon and John Dory – with chips of course!

Friday, 22 June – Meeting 9.30 a.m. Travelled to Sydney Football Stadium. This is my first visit to the stadium and I'm quite impressed. The ground is compact and it looks like it will be a good atmosphere. I will be starting the game because Dan is injured. It's a massive shame for him because he has only just got over an injury sustained with England, against Wales. He is a very good player and has been in fine form. For this to happen a week before the First Test match is cruel. He seems to be handling it very well but I'm sure he will be feeling it inside. He joins a growing list of players having to leave the tour party, including Simon Taylor, Phil Greening and Mike Catt – three out of four of them got injured in

151

training. A few of the players who have left have joined up with the touring supporters.

I spent most of the afternoon on the beach just chilling.

Saturday, 23 June – NSW Waratahs. This was a physical game with the Waratahs trying all sorts to put us off. It was intense from the off and we showed good discipline. We managed to score early on with them having a man in the sin bin. I managed to score two on the night, taking my tally to eight in four games. I am pleased with my performance, not just in attack but in defence. Duncan McRae was sent off for getting stuck into Ronan O'Gara. [He later received a seven-match ban.] Lions 41–24.

Sunday, 24 June – Travelled to Coffs Harbour. I have not been picked for the game on Tuesday and I must admit I'm quite relieved after playing the last four games in the space of eleven days. I'm rooming with Iain Balshaw for the next three days. Balsh hasn't had many opportunities to show what he's capable of but I'm sure that will come.

Monday, 25 June – Today was a tragic day with the news that Anton, the team's kitman, had died. I was in the lobby when I found out he'd had a heart attack, but I didn't realise he had died. He had been out in a boat on a whale-watching trip with some of the boys. They were coming back when Anton decided to swim to shore from about 150 metres out. Although he was fifty-two he was very fit and used to be a lifeguard. He got halfway to shore when he waved to let the boys know he was all right. At that point, they left in the boat. It must have been soon after that that he got into difficulties. He had a heart attack in the water and was pulled out of the sea by some young surfers who noticed something bobbing about in the water.

I walked down to the beach and the police and ambulance were there. I just couldn't believe it. I was talking to him only the other day about his family and how he came to live in Australia. Anton was a lovely man who would do anything for you. He always had a smile on his face and loved his job. He will be sadly missed by many people. I sat down near the beach and thought about how life can be taken in a split-second. It's times like this that really put life into perspective. It got me thinking about my own family and how we should make the most of what we have and the time we spend together. By the time I got back to the hotel, the news had spread. There was an atmosphere of shock and a sense of great loss. God bless Anton.

Tuesday, 26 June – NSW Country Cockatoos. The players who were not playing had training this morning and then got ready to go to the game – 3 p.m. kick-off. The game was poor – the ref was shocking. At times it was embarrassing just watching. The good thing to come out of it was our defence. This was the best defence to date with only a few missed tackles. Lawrence Dallaglio had to pull out through injury and will not play another game on tour.

Wednesday, 27 June – During our team meeting the team for the First Test was announced and my name was there. It was great news. This will be my first start in a Test match. We had a training session followed by a media session. I found myself at the centre of attention and had to do many interviews and photos. We left for Brisbane that evening, flying on two thirty-two-seater planes. I found out I was rooming with Rob Henderson again – no chance! I managed to get a room on my own, but stayed with Amanda tonight on the Gold Coast. It gave me a chance to see her and the kids, and we have tomorrow morning off.

Thursday, 28 June – I took Jemimah and Cameron to the games room. Jemimah and and I raced Cameron on the Sega rally car game. Cameron's very good on this sort of game. We went for a walk around the local shops afterwards, and a car veered off the road at the side of us and ran into a lamp-post, about seven feet from where we had been walking. The man inside seemed to be having some sort of seizure and a few people ran to his aid. I thanked the Lord for keeping us safe.

We joined David, Lynne, Melanie, Heather and Amanda for lunch in their hotel. When I tried to book a taxi to take me back to my hotel, they said they couldn't get one in time, but they had a limousine that would take me for less than a taxi. I didn't want to go back in a stretch-limo but I had no choice. I asked the driver to pull up short of the hotel entrance so that no one would see me getting out. Thankfully, no one did. We trained and had the evening off.

Friday, 29 June – We had a meeting this morning and were then being taken by coach to the Gabba. It had started to rain so I decided to get my waterproofs from the room. I must have been slow because the coach went without me. There were some fans in the foyer who realised what had happened and they insisted on giving me some cash for a taxi. I arrived just after the team and mixed in with everyone as if nothing had happened – nobody had realised I was missing. I had a laugh with a few people about that.

We had the afternoon off and were told to get some rest. There are loads of fans staying in the hotel so it's best not to show your face too much in the foyer. It's good to mix with the fans but hard to escape. The Queensland State of Origin rugby league team are staying in our hotel, so there are lots of players knocking about. I saw Wendell Sailor in the lift and spoke to Wayne Bennett.

Saturday, 30 June – Australia, First Test. We met in the afternoon. The forwards did a few lineouts, the backs just talked through a few of our plays. Later, our shirts were presented to us by Willie-John McBride, a former Lions great. He gave a short talk about the Lions' history and what this game meant to everyone. As we went downstairs to get on the coach, we passed through the lobby and it was full of fans. I could tell more than ever how important this match was going to be.

At the Gabba we did our warm-up in a large room under the stand. As the intensity was building up inside, we were unaware of just how much it was building up outside. When we went out, the first thing I noticed was a sea of red shirts. The noise was deafening.

We responded by starting the game really well. Within two minutes I found myself in a one-on-one situation with the full-back, Chris Latham. I chose to take him on the outside with only a metre or so of room to work with. He must have thought I was coming back on the inside, so before he could react I was round him. I managed to stay just inside the touchline to run in and score the first try. It felt great. We went on to play some great rugby and win the game.

We are thrilled with the result but there are two more Tests and I'm sure Australia will be a lot tougher to beat next time. Lions 29, Australia 13.

Sunday, 1 July to Wednesday, 4 July – Blank diary.

Thursday, 5 July – Day off in Melbourne. John Forbes from Puma picked me up and we went to the Puma HQ to meet some people and collect some stash.

This evening I went to watch Melbourne Storm play the Tigers at Colonial Stadium – venue for the Second Test. As I was leaving for the game, I was reminded by NTL that I was supposed to do a live web chat over the phone. I didn't feel much like doing it, especially on my day off, but I agreed to do it at the game while watching the rugby. The chat turned out to be a long-winded affair, with it taking a long time for them to type in my answers to all the questions being asked. I left the stadium feeling tired and disappointed with the game I had just watched, Melbourne winning by 50 or so points.

The only good thing to come out of the night was the fact that I liked the feel of the stadium. With the roof closed, it created a great atmosphere and that was with just 10,000 Aussies in. When our supporters get in there and sing their hearts out, the place will be bouncing.

Friday, 6 July – We had our final session before the Second Test. It went well but I was still having problems with my Achilles. We had the afternoon off but could not leave the hotel because of the huge number of fans. It's getting that bad that we've got to avoid reception or any other public area in the hotel. This restricts you to the team room or your bedroom.

Amanda is coming to the game. I've sorted out her transport to and from the airport and the match.

Saturday, 7 July – Australia, Second Test. Another long day spent waiting around for the kick-off. Amanda arrived at 3.15 p.m. and I was able to see her for an hour before going to the pre-match meeting. She came downstairs to watch the fans' reaction as we boarded the bus to the game. As soon as we came out of the meeting room, the fans started singing and shouting at the tops of their voices. The hotel foyer was bouncing. I've never seen away support like this in all my life. It was brilliant. Amanda told me later it brought a tear to her eye and I must admit it made the hairs on the back of my neck stand on end.

We arrived at the stadium full of confidence and ready to play. The first half went quite well although we failed to finish the chances we created. We led 11–6 but we knew we had to come out and play much better in the second half. Within four minutes they got an interception and scored a try. Shortly after that they scored again, which put them in the lead for the first time. We seemed to lose focus for about ten minutes and the Aussies were back in the game. We failed to get field position and they put us under pressure. We made a few mistakes and turned over a lot of ball. It was a disappointing end to a game we controlled in the first half. The Aussies won by 21 points.

I met Amanda afterwards and we had a meal together in the hotel. I was pleased she had come all that way to see me play. Her flight back to the Gold Coast leaves at 6 a.m.

Sunday, 8 July – Did a pool session in the morning with Blackie before going out for lunch with some of the boys. It was Neil Jenkins' birthday, so we spent time with him. On the flight to Sydney, I asked a flight attendant if they could announce his birthday over the intercom. I told them he was thirty-six instead of twenty-nine. David Wallace also had his birthday today so we gave him a mention as well.

I had two hours' sleep last night so I was feeling extremely tired. I went round to catch up with Amanda and the kids.

Monday, 9 July to Tuesday, 10 July – Blank diary.

Wednesday, 11 July – Can't remember much about today other than going to Ribs and Rumps again with the family – or rather, I'm trying not to remember. After training this morning I went to the dentist with Iain Balshaw, both of us suffering from a similar problem. I had a crown at the back that was loose and found out that the tooth underneath was broken. The dentist took the crown off, then had to take part of my tooth away. I left the dentist relieved that the problem had been sorted out but nursing a numb jaw.

Thursday, 12 July – We went to Stadium Australia (venue for the Third Test and home of the Sydney Olympics 2000) this morning and it was great to think that I would be playing in such a huge ground in two days' time. After lunch I phoned Amanda and she was having problems with Cameron. I went round to help. He went to sleep OK and his behaviour is improving. When I left all was quiet.

Friday, 13 July – After training, I went to get my hair cut at the same place as last time and was greeted in the shop by an Irish fan. I went back to the hotel to hibernate for thirty hours. It's great to see so many supporters but I'm worn out with all the attention I'm getting.

Later, I challenged Drisco [Brian O'Driscoll] to a table-tennis match. I know that he's better than me, but I'm determined to beat him two games on the trot. Why do men have to be so competitive in all they do? I don't know but I can't help it. He won the first game, I won the second, and in the third he beat me by three points. I was quite pleased to get that close. We retired to the room for a hot chocolate before going to sleep.

Saturday, 14 July – Australia, Third Test. Austin [Healey] had to pull out with a bulging disc in his back and we were short of cover at number 9. Andy Nicol – in Australia with the supporters – was brought in as cover. Dafydd took Austin's place and Andy was on the bench, which left Mark Taylor having to drop out of the squad. That was a decision that must have been hard to swallow. We had our walk through as usual and headed back to base.

It was an hour's bus ride to the game. We had our meeting in the changing room and everyone seemed ready for the challenge ahead. During the warm-up, I got poked in the right eye and was struggling to focus for five or ten minutes in the first half. I'm just glad they didn't kick a 'bomb' early on.

After a few penalty kicks were exchanged, I managed to score the first try in the left-hand corner. That took my tally to ten tries in seven games. It was an easy score. I just had to catch the ball and run five yards over the line. We went to half-time trailing by just three points (13–16) but confident. I don't think there was any big thing we did wrong except the odd turnover. We trailed by six points in the last four minutes and put them under huge pressure near their line. We had one last throw of the dice but failed to secure the ball at a lineout on their line. Australia had won the series. So near yet so far away . . . very disappointing.

But on a personal note, this tour has gone really well for me — from my debut scoring five tries to scoring the first try in the First and Third Tests. The Lord has once again been very good to me on and off the field. I've been able to speak with the players like I've never done before, and I'm grateful to all the people who have prayed for me over the past two months.

Sunday, 15 July – I woke up this morning very sore, having had a knock just above my right knee. I had an MRI scan to make sure there was no ligament damage. I also had a scan on my left wrist and right hand. Everything came back negative.

I had lunch with Brian Kennedy and Ian Blackhurst, overlooking the bay at Manly, before getting ready to fly to Cairns for a family holiday. It's been a long time coming, and I'm really looking forward to it. Having played the rugby league season through the summer 2000, I went straight into the rugby union season. The Third Test was my sixtieth game in a year. My body is in pieces. If I never see a rugby ball again it won't bother me!

Win, lose or draw I suppose there was always going to be an inquest into the Lions tour. For me, it was a great experience but the hardest two months of rugby in my life – a lot of travelling and a lot of training with not a lot of down time. I felt like a zombie most of the time, and I was not alone, I can assure you. It was a shame really because, had we been fresh, I think we could have won all three Test matches.

The management had to integrate a host of players who were strangers to one another as fast and as successfully as they could. Time was always going to be the enemy. But it never seemed to make sense to have full-contact training sessions the day after a game, for example. We sustained a lot of injuries in training and, having spoken with others since the tour, it seems the treatment of some players was unfair. Some had given their all on tour and were left to fend for themselves after they had been injured, including Dan Luger, Mike Catt and Phil Greening. If they wanted to go home, fine, but if they wanted to stay, they should have been looked after.

It was a hard grind. In hindsight, I suspect Graham Henry and the other coaching staff would do things differently although they were obviously doing what they thought best at the time.

The fans were amazing and there seemed to be Welsh people, in particular, everywhere. It has to be the only time in their lives they will ever cheer an Englishman! The Australians just didn't realise how much support we would receive. They were stunned into retaliation by the Third Test, and gave away free scarves for that game and coloured every seat in Stadium Australia gold and green, or so it seemed.

After seven weeks, we came up one game short. We were probably a bit stale; certainly we weren't fresh. But had we won that lineout on the Australian line and scored near the end of the game, all would have be forgotten. When Australian lock Justin Harrison stole our throw at the front of the line, I felt utterly deflated. Hopefully, lessons will have been learned from the tour. I am sure the management set-up will be different for the next venture and it will be noted that, coming off the back of a domestic season of rugby, it is not fitness you are lacking.

At the end of the Sydney Test, there were tired and disappointed men in the Lions dressing room. From day one we had wanted to be the best there ever was. Now we had lost and it had all been in vain. Yet Donal Lenihan walked into our dressing room and spoke to us with passion. He gave an emotional speech of gratitude, unashamedly crying as he thanked the players for their efforts from the bottom of his heart. He told us that it had been a pleasure for him to have been involved with us. He was hurting with us.

I will never forget being a Lion. Everyone assumed before the tour that I would be used as an auxiliary weapon, a man to come off the bench in bad times or good times. But I made it into the starting team for the Tests, and I scored tries across Australia although I am the first to admit that the try scorer usually gets more than his share of credit. Too often people are blind to the guy who has had his nose broken in winning the ball for you.

But we did not get the job done to our satisfaction. As Donal spoke in our deathly quiet dressing room in Stadium Australia, I could relate to his tears. I could feel his pain mingling with my own.

Heartache on a more personal level struck in the autumn of 2001, not long after I came home from the Lions tour. My brother George was sent to prison for drug-related offences.

At first I was reluctant to visit him because I was worried what the newspapers would print if they got hold of the story. I am appalled to admit that even now. My brother was behind bars and all I cared about was my image. Thankfully, I came to my senses and realised that I was wrong. For a start, his name is Brannan and he's white. The chances of strangers making a connection were remote, but so what if they did?

I had never visited anyone in prison before so I was extremely surprised when Mum told me to bring my passport with me for ID. Before you can get into the jail, you have to go through a rigorous inspection. You have to place your hand in a machine to have your fingerprints photographed. Your hand is stamped, you fill out various forms, and finally you pass through a security arch like the ones they have at airports. Obviously, they are trying to prevent people from bringing drugs into the prison.

Once inside, you are shown to a waiting room and someone shouts down for the prisoner you have come to visit. There is little privacy as you sit round a table with others. I was recognised and embarrassed when people came over to ask for my autograph. It felt like the wrong place and the wrong time to be signing autographs. I didn't want the unnecessary attention.

While it is desperately sad to see your brother in jail, as a family we felt a great deal of relief when he was locked up. He was so heavily into drugs, he was lucky to be alive. Three times he was rushed to hospital after overdosing; only the swift attention of medics saved his life.

George's fall into drug addiction was an enormous shock. I always remembered him being so anti-drugs when we were growing up. He despised any of his friends who took them. Yet somehow George got involved, and he fell into a deeper and deeper abyss from 1999 until, finally, he was sent down in 2001. Heroin took over his life.

To be truthful, I did not know to what extent he had become addicted, as Mum didn't tell me all she knew. She carried the burden by herself. She did not want to worry me or for me to be involved. Only later did I discover the level of strain she had been under. It almost killed her. George and I used to talk on the telephone, but the more he became dependent on drugs, and he was selling them to make money to feed his own habit, the less communicative he became. I'd phone home and if he answered the phone, he would say, 'I'll just get Mum,' and that was all. At one point, I tried to sort out a place for him at a Christian rehabilitation clinic but he was not interested in seeking real help. Heroin had messed up his head big time.

One day, Mum started crying on the phone and I immediately drove to Leeds to support her. We went to the house where George lived with his girlfriend. I was not prepared for what I saw. George had always taken a lot of pride in the way he looked. He dressed smartly and wore good shoes. Now he was sitting on his bed with my mum's pyjamas on. I was distraught. He had lost so much weight he looked to be at death's door. He looked like an old man and I thought, 'That's my brother.'

He was at a stage where he was lying all the time. He told me, 'Jason, I can't help it. I lie to get what I need.' George wasn't fit to work. He had money coming in from selling drugs, but the money was vanishing just as fast as it arrived as he bought the drugs he needed. He was sucked into a desperately vicious circle. He would be crying in pain, hurting too much to move. When George was finally locked up, it was a real blessing in disguise. He entered a voluntary testing unit because, according to George, drugs are rife in prison.

It was right that George was imprisoned. He always said if you can't do the time, don't do the crime. There were times when he felt suicidal. We all visited him, but, of course, time was passing slowly for him. He had lost touch with the outside world and he could not understand how busy I was, or how busy our brother Bernard was. Bernard has always worked all hours. He works for a company dealing with asbestos removal and he has a wife and two children, a girl and a boy.

In prison, George hopefully began to think what he might do in life. He was released in September 2002 and he seems positive and upbeat. He is seeing his daughter again, finding purpose and direction in his life. I think more than anything he wants to make it up to Mum. He realises it has affected everyone around him.

Tragically, drugs took the life of my cousin Lisa when she was only twenty-one years old. We all really love George and we do not want to lose him as well.

13

NATIONAL SERVICE

'You have reached the pinnacle of success as soon as you become uninterested in money, compliments or publicity.'

EDDIE RICKENBACKER

Before I was selected for the Lions, I had my first taste of international rugby union with England at the outset of 2001. I confess I was like a new boy at school when I reported to Pennyhill Park in Bagshot, the hotel complex where England coach Clive Woodward has established the squad's headquarters. One of the reasons for switching to rugby union was to get this opportunity.

Once at Pennyhill Park, I could not help but be impressed by the professionalism of the set-up. There is a rugby pitch in the grounds with a second one planned, I understand. There is a fitness centre and a nine-hole golf course. The management cater for the players' every whim. My slight disadvantage to begin with was that I just didn't know too many of the other players, by sight or name! My career and my thoughts had always been with rugby league and it just shows you how much I didn't know about this game. People must have thought when I stressed this that it was an overstatement, but it was the truth.

As a player joining up with a squad of strangers, I hoped to be judged on my performance. As a person, I hoped to be judged by the manner in which I conducted myself. No doubt some had heard stories about my past; stories go about quicker than I ever did, especially the ones you don't want to get out. But from the start I was made welcome.

I was surprised at how many of the players were into rugby league. I soon discovered that Jonny Wilkinson and Martin Johnson had great knowledge of the game. In general, the guys loved watching the Super League on Friday nights. For my part, I was just determined to make the most of the chance on offer. I'd been a professional long enough to know what it takes to play at the highest level – not just on the pitch, but how to prepare mentally and physically. Clive Woodward is the one who thought I might make the grade at rugby union and I have reason to be grateful to him for backing his intuition. It is appropriate to hear what Clive feels about how I responded to my new environment rather than just my take on the switch:

In Jason's first England session, you could see he added a spark to the whole training. That was the beauty of bringing in somebody with his own ideas on how to play the game. Rugby union was changing dramatically. We needed more and more players who could beat people one on one. Just to see Jason's speed and footwork was exhilarating. Jonny Wilkinson observed in his book *Lions and Falcons* that from the moment the players saw Jason's footwork and his change of pace, everybody went, 'Crikey, we are behind.' They didn't need me to tell them, and off Jonny went to start working hard on his own footwork. That's the standard we have to get to, then get past.

We always encourage note-taking in team meetings, but as soon as Jason sat down, he was really taking notes. I was watching him, the players were watching him. Before we started a training session, he'd be out there almost fifteen minutes before everybody else, preparing himself. He was setting examples for us all. You can't overstress this. The game of rugby union was amateur until 1997, but Jason had been a professional in league for nearly ten years. What we could take from him was the way he operated. He moved things on to a new level in so many ways.

After my crash-course introduction to the international set-up I was selected as a substitute for England's opening match in the Six Nations championship against Italy because Dan Luger was injured. As the coach neared Twickenham, the sense of occasion struck me. People waved and shouted encouragement as our bus passed them. Once inside the ground, I found there was a plaque in the dressing room with my name on it. Each player has a long bench with vertical sides making it a cubicle. I looked again at my name. It felt special. I was part of an ambitious squad, a group of talented and highly focused individuals, but I still had a lot of hard work to do to get into the team. I was willing to watch, learn and wait for my chance.

England controlled the game as you would expect from a team with so much experience and drive. Then, with something like fifteen minutes to go, the message I hoped for was passed to me. I was to go on. As I prepared myself, a lot of thoughts swirled around my head. This was it, this was the moment I would become an England international at rugby union. How would the fans react? What would they think of this guy from rugby league? Are they going to get behind me or are they going to be critical?

I was itching to play, to show what I could do in the white

shirt with the red rose. Thankfully, my arrival at the side of the pitch coincided with a roar of approval. I felt even more excited. It seemed everyone was as impatient as I was to see me with the ball. But it was one of those afternoons when nothing quite went for me. I had licence to cover the pitch, but no matter where I went the ball never got there. I might have touched the ball twice in total. Sure, it was a little disappointing, but I accepted it for what it was; just one of those things.

Later, there were suggestions flying around that I had been deliberately denied any decent ball to put me down. That was nonsense, of course. We play a professional game in a professional age and there is not a player in the England squad who is anything but committed to the ethos of the team. As I say, it was one of those days when the harder I looked for the ball, the more difficult it was to find. There can always be days like that. Ask any winger. It was only commented on because there had been a lot of hype around my debut.

I realised there was still much to learn, but I knew that this was the stage on which I wanted to perform. I was used as a substitute for the next two England games, against Scotland and France, and I'm glad I was introduced like that. It eased me into the scene. Of course, when I made it on to the Lions tour of Australia that summer, commentators leapt on the storyline of me winning a Lions Test debut before I had started a game for England. That happened as a matter of circumstance, not as a matter of planning, I can assure you.

After the Lions returned home that summer, disappointed and wondering what might have been, England had to play Ireland in October in the climax of the previous winter's Six Nations championship. The original fixture had been postponed due to the restrictions imposed because of the dreadful foot and mouth disease that brought so much misery to farmers. With the Grand Slam beckoning for England, I was chosen to begin the game on the wing. We lost – Ireland claiming a victory that will grow in legend with the passing years. We had not played as a team for over six months and, no matter how hard you work on the training pitch, there really is no substitute for playing. We made mistakes and the Irish played with typical hunger and desire against us. Nothing seems to make them more determined to succeed than the sight of a white jersey. It is a tale other England players have recounted over the years. It is also the truth. On the day, Ireland would not be denied, and the Grand Slam dream perished.

My next game for England was at Twickenham against world champions Australia – at full-back. There was general surprise from those outside the game that I was selected in that position, but I felt I was equipped to fulfil what was being asked of me. So did Clive, who explains why he chose to switch me from the wing:

In the England games before the Lions tour, we hammered Wales, Italy, Scotland and France. Those four games produced the best rugby I have seen from any England team at any level. Jason came on in the last three and made a fantastic impact. After we played Scotland – and they played well but we still got 40-odd points on them – scrum-half Andy Nicol said, 'I couldn't believe it, we're out on our feet and then I saw Jason Robinson take his tracksuit off.' Jason destroyed them for the last twenty minutes. Then he went on the Lions tour and got fast-tracked even quicker. I was delighted he was chosen for the Lions team because exposure to the game at the highest levels helped with his development. When he scored that try in the First Test in Brisbane – and I was there working for Sky Sports – it was one of those moments when you get to your feet and go potty. It was brilliant to see that he could do something like that against arguably the best defensive team in the world. No one touched him. I was watching him all the time and thinking, this guy can play full-back. Every time he touched the ball he was lethal.

And then, of course, England had the disaster against Ireland in Dublin, where Jason played from the start on the wing with Iain Balshaw at full-back. We'd had six months off as a team and I was still picking players based on how they were playing for me in April, and I got a few things wrong. Balshaw had obviously lost a lot of confidence on the Lions tour.

So I had to move quickly and take a big positive step, not go backwards. The big positive step was putting Jason at full-back against world champions Australia in our next game at Twickenham. I always thought this could be his best position.

This was not a view shared by members of the press. At the press conference after the team was announced, they kept asking me what I would do if the Australians tried me out under a high ball. I told them part of the plan was that I would catch it. When I told Clive, he practically fell over laughing. I've got a pretty good standing jump – three feet – which takes me higher than most guys six feet tall can jump. I don't drop the ball very often, and I'd been practising my kicking, so I can do it when I have to.

In the game, first chance they got, the Australians kicked to me. I made the catch, and beat the first two defenders. They kept kicking to me because they thought I had a weakness, and all of Twickenham was screaming, 'Kick it to Robinson, kick it to Robinson,' because they wanted me to have the ball and run it back at the Aussies. After twenty minutes, everyone was laughing – Clive, the fans, the press, me. It was unbelievable.

I really enjoyed the game against the Australians and it was good to be on the winning side against them so soon after the shattering disappointment of the Lions' defeat in the decisive Third Test in July. Every game was still a learning curve, but I have always been able to catch a rugby ball since I was a kid. Other factors had to be worked on. The more I played the more I realised how different a game it was from league. There were some things I got to grips with early, such as placing the ball back in the tackle. I'd been used to holding on to the ball, now I had to make certain my presentation of the ball was good. I'd done a lot of work on that in training, and my club helped me.

Clive, on the other hand, was worried about over-coaching. This is what he said:

> Coach contact skills and kicking skills, but his ability to read the game and find holes – well, you leave that to him and cover for him. I'm coaching the best players in the country and I think the way we play suits him. We'll keep hold of the ball and wait for him; basically, he's just got to spot the breaks. His support play is excellent, but I don't understand those who believe he belongs on the wing. He is far better served being that last guy. The next part of his game development is to start kicking a little more. But when you've got players such as Ben Cohen and Dan Luger outside him, if he starts running and makes his pass . . .

I was determined to play no differently from the way I had played for Wigan. I thought it was my best chance of making an impact. I don't claim to be the best or the fastest; I'm just different. I like to play on the edge. I take a lot of risks, especially with my desire to bring the ball back. I don't want to appear arrogant, but I think it's made a lot of people aware of other possibilities. Teams, generally, are playing a more expansive game. The shape of the average rugby union player is changing all the time. Players are stronger, faster and fitter. Your average prop forward – without wishing to cause any offence – used to be a funny shape. He was designed to amble from one scrum to the next – not any more, though, certainly not in the top echelons of the game. Nowadays, props get around the pitch, handle the ball and make a great number of tackles. Players have worked extremely hard on their fitness. You have some back-row men who can outpace three-quarters. That's scary.

That autumn series – against Australia, Romania and South Africa – spread a feel-good factor within the England squad and we went into the Six Nations championship in 2002 feeling optimistic. Regrettably, our chances of the Grand Slam perished again. This time France beat us, deservedly so, in Paris, and won the Slam, another bitter pill we had to swallow. We had promised much as a team and, again, we had come up one game short. Yet there remained a sense of optimism. There was more right than wrong with England's rugby. Once the disappointment of the moment had passed, I am sure, like me, the other players in the squad looked forward to the future with optimism, keen to rise to the fresh challenges ahead.

At club level, the 2001–02 season was a real success for Sale. The club won the Parker Pen Shield, defeating Pontypridd in the final, and finished runners-up in the Zurich Premiership after finishing third from bottom in the previous year. Jim

Mallinder and Steve Diamond, both in their first year in charge, deserve much credit. Here were two former Sale players given a tough job and, like the rest of the boys, they had a lot to learn in their new role. Jim and Steve worked hard at creating a good atmosphere at the club. Team spirit was one of our strongest assets. We all wanted the club to succeed, and I think our results showed the strength of our determination and dedication.

I was named player of the season, a humbling experience when you think it was my first full year in rugby union. I cannot do justice in words to how welcome I have been made at Sale. From day one, everyone at the club has been great. Brian Kennedy is a superb chairman. He is easy to be around, not slow to have a laugh, but we know where to draw the line with him. He cares passionately for the club.

I was relieved to get a holiday in the summer of 2002 as, apart from that short family holiday in Australia after the Lions tour, I had played virtually non-stop for two years. I am a fan of hitting the open road and I hitched up a caravan for us to tour Devon and Cornwall. It was good for the spirit, good to be with Amanda and the children. Some of the sites we stayed at were just farmer's fields. One night I was awoken at 4 a.m. by the sound of a bleating sheep circling our caravan. It had found its way on to the site from a neighbouring field – I just had to laugh. All in all, it was a great holiday. I am no stranger to taking holidays in a caravan; it was what I did as a child. Sometimes the simple things in life are more important than jetting off to the sun. To my mind, location is not the important factor. The important thing is spending time with the family, when they come first and there are no interruptions involving work of any kind. Going to another country is not the only way to unwind – although I probably wouldn't turn down a couple of weeks in the Maldives!

The only trouble with good holidays is that they seem to end too soon. Before we knew, it was time for pre-season training; and there was the additional commitment of preparing for England's autumn series with New Zealand, Australia and South Africa. After years of the club versus country debate, Clive Woodward had created an environment in which he was able to call up players from their clubs to join England for a succession of training camps at Pennyhill Park. Clive and his coaches, Andy Robinson, Phil Larder, Dave Alred, Simon Hardy and Phil Keith-Roche, leave little to chance. For someone like me, living so far north, this entailed a lot of extra days away from home. I needed to leave home around teatime to report to Pennyhill Park by Sunday evening. With Amanda pregnant with our third child, the days I had to spend training with England were hard on her, but they were a necessity if I wanted to be an international – and I did. I wanted to be in contention for the World Cup in Australia in October and November 2003.

We worked hard in those training sessions, starting on Monday mornings and parting company late each Tuesday afternoon. Even though we managed something like twenty days together as a squad, you can never be sure how you will perform as a team until you get on the pitch on match day. As New Zealand were our first opponents, we knew our rehearsals had to be near word-perfect or we would be made to look foolish when the curtain rose at Twickenham.

The All Blacks do not come to England that often, and everyone wanted a ticket for the game. I was especially excited about playing against them – Jonah Lomu and all. John Mitchell, who had previously been an England coach alongside Clive, coaches the All Blacks these days. As a Kiwi, Mitchell had jumped at the chance to return home. When he chose his party to tour, Mitchell had left behind some of the All Blacks' top performers, arguing they needed a rest after a hard domestic season. Still, New Zealand arrived with a more than handy squad.

It seems that Lomu had been subjected to a great deal of criticism in New Zealand, his form reportedly indifferent by their high standards. Mitchell declared that Lomu was the only one of his party not selected on merit. By inference, he was in England on his reputation. What clever psychology by the All Blacks coach! What more motivation do you need as a player, once you have been told in public that you are only in the team on reputation?

That reputation included running England into the ground in a World Cup match in South Africa in 1995, of course. We might have guessed he would have a big match against England at Twickenham. Lomu is an amazing athlete. You don't meet that many men his size with his speed. He is like a tower block running at you. Jonah scored two tries, reminding the rugby world that he was far from a spent force. I made a last-ditch attempt to tackle him when he went down the outside, but as he was more or less jumping over the line as I arrived there was no chance to stop him scoring.

Of course, it was an ideal stage for him to bounce back. He'd had illness, he'd had a loss of form and he'd been harshly criticised for not being the player he was of old. Even though he knows he can win games, this had been a big burden for him to carry and so Twickenham was an important occasion for Jonah.

Similarly, it was critical for England. Mitchell had claimed beforehand that he was putting out a depleted team, which was all part of the legendary All Blacks psychological warfare. If they lost, Mitchell had a ready-made excuse; if they won, he could say victory had been achieved without their strongest side being on the field. He had created a no-lose situation for New Zealand's rugby-obsessed population.

Our agenda dealt in the here and now. Our coaches made it plain that our first objective was to win the game. If we won in style, that would be a bonus. Tries from Lewis Moody, Jonny Wilkinson and Ben Cohen, as well as two conversions and three penalties from Jonny, gave England victory by 31–28. We held out against a fierce finish from the All Blacks.

Our objective had been achieved, but there was plenty of room for improvement. Under the incessant urgency of back-to-back matches, we had precious little time to polish our game plan for the next one, against Australia. I think we all knew that we had to approach that game differently. I kicked the ball too many times against the All Blacks. I am not there to kick. All right, there are times when I must, but for the match with the Australians, I had to have a different mindset.

We did have to take into account that the All Blacks game was our first as a team for six months. Although we'd had team sessions, it is hard to know what level you are at until you play a big-pressure game against some of the best players in the world. Nothing really prepares you for that, but that doesn't mean you don't try to be prepared as best you can.

Everyone wanted to make out it was a depleted All Blacks

team – but when did a New Zealand rugby team play without heart, passion and a blinding desire to win? No one without those qualities was ever handed a black jersey. The team chosen to play against us knew the responsibility they had to uphold. Some first-choice players may have remained at home, but the team that they fielded was still a strong one.

We want to play a style of rugby that doesn't let up for one minute. We want to pressure the opposition at all times and, hopefully, they won't be able to live with us.

With victory over the All Blacks, the public's expectation level was cranked up another notch. As the Wallabies had lost in Dublin on the same afternoon as we beat the All Blacks, England fans arrived at Twickenham with tails high. Within the squad, however, the result from Ireland served to ring alarm bells. We knew these Wallabies were nursing wounded pride – and a wounded animal is a dangerous beast.

What a game it turned out to be! We dominated, we led, we were overhauled and we went behind – but we never panicked, we never lost our shape and we showed the Australians that this generation of England players competes until the final whistle. We won 32–31, and it is fair to assume that our comeback stunned the Wallabies.

Martin Johnson is an England captain with a calculating mind. He kept the team focused, with one eye on the big electronic clock, one eye on the game plan. His message to the team was plain – if Australia can rack up points in no time, so can we. When you are behind and the clock is against you, it is easy to panic and stray from the game plan. We stuck to the task and, in doing so, staged a comeback that had never before been achieved against a team of the stature of Australia, the reigning world champions. I had lost to Australia numerous times in my career and there was an enormous sense of satisfaction in winning a game from a losing position against them. It's games like this that illustrate how far you have come as a team.

The next morning Stephen Jones reported in the *Sunday Times*:

This is becoming an autumn of rugby heroics. England emerged from a match of imperfections but stunning entertainment with a victory that was tiny in its statistics but massively well deserved.

They won because they were the more incisive side but also because, crucially, they kept their nerve and their shape after subsiding to 31–19 down after 56 minutes – this after a calamitous period either side of half-time that brought Australia's world champions 25 points in 17 minutes.

At that stage, it seemed that, yet again, a British rugby team was in grave danger of making the current bunch of Australians look the outstanding team they emphatically are not. The British Lions know the feeling. England had a clear edge in the forward play and in terms of ambition. However, not only was England's defence hair-raisingly shaky at key times, but their tactical kicking game was even worse and none of Jonny Wilkinson, Mike Tindall and Will Greenwood can escape blame.

They also lacked finishing power in the first half when their approach work created enough space for them to score at least three or four more tries. But considering that some important parts of England's game were misfiring, and the profound possibilities for improvement, they can be thrilled with their victory. Two southern-hemisphere towers demolished, South Africa to come on Saturday. Yesterday, we saw giants such as Martin Johnson, Richard Hill and Phil Vickery restored to full steaming, we saw some electric

breaks around the fringes from Matt Dawson and another perform-
ance of wonderful courage and enterprise from Jason Robinson.
England's points came from two world-class scoring machines. Ben
Cohen scored twice and played superbly.

There was also brilliant goal-kicking from Wilkinson, who scored
22 points. Some of his generalship and organisation was not of the
best, but there are a good few players about who would settle for
an off-day like that.

Critically, what shone through on this extraordinary afternoon
was the character of the England team. When we had fallen
behind, maybe the Australians were anticipating the floodgates
would open. Perhaps there was an anxiety among the England
supporters, too. Had England not fallen under the force of Irish
pressure at Lansdowne Road? But on the pitch, we were aware
of the pitfalls. We were determined not to force a pass when
no opportunity existed. We reminded each other to be patient.
We wanted to exert pressure on the Wallabies and that was what
we did. We wore down Australia, respected as masters of
defence. Fear is a factor that works in your favour at moments
like this. You are afraid to be a liability to the team. You are
afraid to get caught and allow the other team to turn over the
ball. Through fear, you find the courage to apply yourself, your
mind hard and sharp and clear of distraction.

Attention to detail is important, too. Early in the match I
found myself falling over. I slipped right in front of the first
Wallaby defender and thought, 'Oh, no.' At half-time I changed
my studs from 18mm to 22mm because I suspected I wasn't
getting any bite from the ground with the shorter ones. That
can be the difference between getting clear and getting caught.
It's the simple things that can make a difference.

There are those who argue that we rely on Jonny Wilkinson's boot too much and there is not a team in the world who would not like a place-kicker of his quality. But here is the reality – if opponents are going to give away penalties, we will take the points Jonny kicks. Penalties are only awarded when rivals are stopping us illegally from playing. Australia were slowing down our ball and got penalised for it. Ideally, we would like to make Jonny redundant and deliver the game we want to play, but that is a pipe-dream. So, while people consistently spoil play, or commit fouls, we will take three points from Jonny and move on.

I have played in teams with good kickers – Frano Botica and Andy Farrell at Wigan, for example – but for all-round ability, Jonny is without equal. By the end of 2002, I ranked Jonny the best all-round player in the world. Not only is he the most accurate kicker in the game, but he can tackle, pass and launch an attack. His skill level is of the highest order. He kicks accurately off both feet, and how many players can do that? When I kick with my left foot, it doesn't feel like my leg is attached to my body! Jonny can throw a pass forty yards, and he's put in some of the biggest defensive hits we have seen.

He has unbelievable vision, bringing a more attacking verve to his game as he grows in confidence. His knowledge of the game is immense. He talks you through how we are going to play, and you rarely see him fazed. He is at the heart of England's strategy from the kick-off. I have no wish to play down anyone else in the team – Clive Woodward has assembled some of the best players in the world today, and you wouldn't want to swap them for anybody – yet everyone involved with England recognises that Jonny is special. It would be easy for him to become self-important, but he is level-headed. He seeks perfection, practising hour after hour, often on his own. If he comes across as a serious-minded young man, totally absorbed by rugby, this is because he takes his responsibilities hard. I also think he is protecting himself from over-exposure in the media.

If Jonny was a soccer player, his value to England would be regarded on a parallel with David Beckham's, but Jonny wouldn't want to be on the celebrity circuit – not that there's anything wrong with being under the spotlight. It's simply a matter of personal preference. Jonny is more like Michael Owen. He likes to keep his private life separate from rugby. The game can raise you up and bring you down, so there has to be a point of reference away from the game that does not move when the pendulum is swinging on the rugby pitch. I have the utmost respect for him.

These were exciting times for English rugby. Supporters were travelling to Twickenham, believing that England would beat these giants from the southern hemisphere. Even with my limited knowledge of the history of the game, I knew that New Zealand, Australia and South Africa had dominated rugby union. With South Africa next, there was a real buzz about the game.

Within the squad, the aim was to keep grounded. After a period of reflection over the Australia match, the emphasis switched to the task ahead. Missing from the Tuesday debrief was Sinbad – James Simpson-Daniel – who had been ill before playing against Australia, and who was now forced to drop out of the reckoning. Clive named another young guy, Phil Christophers, as replacement.

When you arrive at Pennyhill Park for a series such as this, your first concern is wondering if you are to be selected. But once the games have begun, and you are in the team, as I was against New Zealand, you have a better sense of what to expect. You cannot take anything for granted – that would be most unwise – but as long as you don't have a real shocker, you have to believe you will be there or thereabouts when the team for the next game is disclosed to the squad. Clive announces his teams using a flip chart in a team room on the first floor.

Although we are under the microscope with the media and public, this is nothing compared with the scrutiny we come under from the coaching staff. Andy Robinson, forwards coach, and Phil Larder, defensive coach, make detailed points about the previous game. They identify the things we did well and the things we could improve on. They accentuate the positives without ignoring the negatives. At Twickenham, cameras are placed discreetly around the stadium, providing the England coaches with exclusive footage of a match. With this film, they can tell exactly where anyone is at any point in a game. It is like being followed on CCTV in a shopping mall. There is no hiding place – we work in a strictly no-excuse zone.

In addition, statistics are kept to register the contribution of every player. From these stats, you know how many yards you have covered, how fast you ran. It is mindblowing. You can re-trace your part in the match on a computer. Every run, pass, kick or tackle is recorded. Every catch you made, every ruck you hit, every angle you ran and who was covering is placed before you. Welcome to Clive's Big Brother.

The two games with New Zealand and Australia had to be a spectators' dream. Three points separated England from the All Blacks and we finished with a one-point advantage over Australia. Does sport get any better, any more pure as a contest? But these

Right...left...right – an England training session at Sandhurst.

Not exactly 'Ski Sunday' – darting through slalom poles to sharpen footwork during an England session at our training headquarters at Pennyhill Park, Bagshot.

England manager Clive Woodward (*centre*) has surrounded himself with top-class coaches Phil Larder (*left*) and Andy Robinson.

French defenders unsuccessfully trying to push me down a cul-de-sac at Twickenham in February 2001.

Gaining an edge, stealing some ground – I am aiming to keep Australia on the back foot at Twickenham in November 2001.

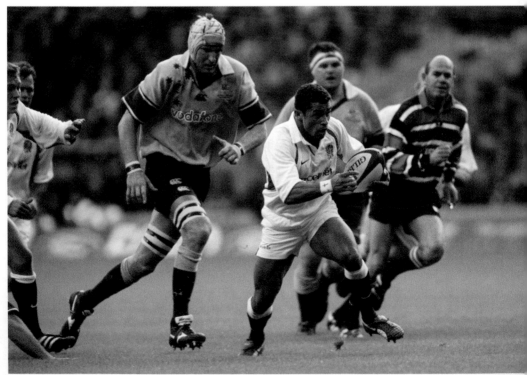

By the time I reached Jonah Lomu, the Big Man was too close to the line for me to deny him a try for New Zealand in November 2002 at Twickenham.

Needing to clear England's lines in the same game against the All Blacks, but in the post-game debrief I felt I had kicked too often.

Jonny Wilkinson, successfully kicking a penalty during the win over New Zealand, is for me the best all-round player in the world.

I might not be the tallest guy on the field, but I know how to jump and catch.

Taking a big hit from South African second-row forward A.J. Venter at Twickenham on 23 November 2002.

Singing the national anthem alongside Jason Leonard (wearing headband), who was making a remarkable 100th appearance in the England front row when we met France at Twickenham on 15 February 2003.

England captain Martin Johnson feels the force of his opposite number, South African Corne Krige. Incidentally, anyone seen the ball?

The Robinson Family: Amanda has Joseph on her knee and Cameron is sitting between Jemimah and me.

Swerving towards the line for one of my two tries for England against Scotland in the 2003 Calcutta Cup.

In an emptying Lansdowne Road stadium, I am wearing Denis Hickie's shirt and a broad grin as England's Grand Slam celebrations begin after the 42–6 win over Ireland in Dublin on 30 March 2003.

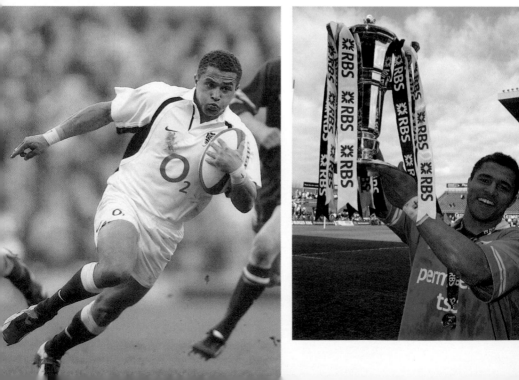

Above Daddy's girl – Jemimah already loves clothes and shoes and will be the perfect shopping partner for her mum!

Right One of my favourite photographs with Amanda.

Below Cameron and Jemimah share an intimate moment with Joseph after his homecoming.

A treasured moment as Cameron reads Jemimah a bedtime story.

Lewis and Cameron play together regularly; here, Cameron is pushing Lewis round the garden.

Building sandcastles on a beach in Devon with Cameron and Jemimah – on holiday in the summer of 2002.

are thoughts that have to be banished. As a player, you cannot fall into the trap of thinking, 'Wow.' As a player, it is not yesterday that is important, it is tomorrow. We knew we could – and had to – get better as a team. We knew that South Africa would present us with a new set of problems, but we did not quite anticipate to what level of desperation they would stoop.

We did not need to be told that it was going to be a tough game. The Springboks had been beaten by France in Paris and by Scotland in Edinburgh and the pressure on them to avoid another defeat must have been immense. We suspected they might target Jonny, scrum-half Matt Dawson and me. I remembered how physical a game it had been when we played them a year earlier when they let me know from the start that I was guaranteed a hard ride.

Now, all of us who play rugby love the physical side of our sport, otherwise we would not be involved. But at Twickenham on 23 November 2002, South Africa's players set out to beat us up. No one can accuse me of sour grapes because we did not lose the game. We scored 53 points, conceded 3, and no South African team has been defeated as badly as that. The shame for South Africa was that, had they channelled their energy into playing rugby, they had the players to compete with us. But all their efforts were focused on stopping England, any way, any how.

I have never seen so many cheap shots in a game. They were guilty of head-butting, throwing late forearm smashes and kicking off the ball. I was butted, hit with a forearm after the ball and, most dangerously of all, kicked in the side of the head when I was standing upright. The kick perforated my right eardrum.

At the time, I had no idea what had happened. It was in the second half, and I went to support Ben Cohen under a high ball. Ben caught the ball and, as can be seen on the video, the South African player kept coming at me after he missed him. The next thing I knew, I had been kicked in the head. It may have been an accident, I suppose, but as I went down, I remember thinking, 'How could I be stood up and yet kicked in the head?' At that instant, I couldn't hear anything other than muffled sounds filling my head. I knew something was wrong because it felt like an explosive device had been detonated in my ear. I lay on the ground motionless. I'm not a hard case but, like most rugby men, I don't stay down out of habit. You have great motivation to stay on the pitch, almost at any cost. I think all of us at the highest level of the game have that same instinct. But sometimes that cussed streak can work to your detriment. There are times when you stay on when, perhaps, it would be wiser to come off.

As I tried to make sense of what was happening, and why I was suddenly deaf in one ear, I was asked a series of questions by the physios. Amid the noise and the fury of Twickenham, they were busily trying to assess my fitness to carry on. You think there is a time limit on how long you can stay down and you tell yourself you must get up. I told the physios there was something wrong with my hearing, but I wasn't angling to be taken off. It's hard enough to hear at Twickenham in any event, so I had to resort to lip-reading and hand signals. I have had bangs on my head before and I was expecting to regain my hearing at any second. Mostly, after a couple of minutes you get back to normal, but this was different. I was dazed and with my hearing impaired my balance was affected. But as I'd taken a bang on my leg, I just dismissed this as the kind of normal soreness you experience in a game of such magnitude. I was always aware of what was going on around me, so I stayed on to finish the job that had been started.

Jonny and Lewis Moody were not as fortunate. Both were injured and had to leave the field. South Africa's Jannes Labuschagne was sent off in the first half for ambushing Jonny with a late tackle, but that was not the challenge that did the damage to him. He was forced out of the game after taking a hit from centre Butch James. His injured left shoulder cost him almost two months of the season for his club, Newcastle.

But for the composure shown by England players, the match could have degenerated into a brawl. New Zealand referee Paddy O'Brien kept telling Martin Johnson, 'Leave it to me, I know what's going on.' Even so, he was not exactly preventing the violent play from being repeated, and there could have been a point when the England players opted to take justice into their own hands. It is a tribute to the team that the players kept cool in the face of extreme provocation. Paul Ackford, a former England second-row forward, filed this scathing condemnation of South Africa in his report for the *Sunday Telegraph* the next morning:

England's autumn of excellence is now confirmed. This was their third important victory against southern-hemisphere opposition, and if the occasion lacked the theatrical majesty of the other two, it was simply because the triumph was a foregone conclusion long before the end. As weary, battle-scarred England trooped off, Twickenham stood in admiration. It has been a sensational three weeks, rugby at its coruscating best, and this area of south-west London will seem very quiet until the arrival of France at the start of the Six Nations.

185

The knockers may point out that England's achievements came at home, where they are now unbeaten in 18 games, and against opposition who are out of season, but only malcontents would deny England significant credit. The side have grown week by week. They can beat only what is placed before them and they will go into phase two of their World Cup build-up with genuine confidence.

South Africa were a shambles, a once proud rugby nation resorting to a litany of late tackles and foul play. It has been a wretched European trip for the Boks, with defeats by France and Scotland, but their humbling by England came close to humiliation. It was always going to be a brutal match. The Springboks have an honourable tradition of physicality taken to the limit, but they lost it yesterday. Lock Jannes Labuschagne was sent off after 22 minutes for a gratuitously late tackle when he drove his shoulder into Jonny Wilkinson's midriff, and there were a number of other unsavoury incidents. The referee, Paddy O'Brien, had no option but to dismiss Labuschagne because at that stage the game was on the verge of anarchy. O'Brien's decision, as courageous as it was appropriate, just about kept the lid on things but, even so, tackles by Corne Krige on Jason Robinson and Richard Hill went far beyond what is acceptable in a collision sport.

Reports after the weekend said Krige spoke to his players behind the goalline as Jonny took aim with his last, lancing kick of the match. Krige told the South African players to freeze these painful memories, and vow to themselves never to experience this kind of hurt again.

That's good and fine, but England players have their own memories. In our dressing room there were men with lumps and bruises, but we were compensated with the reward of a mission accomplished.

When I was seen by one of England's medical staff afterwards, I was told I had a big 'hole' in my ear. On Monday, Sale doctor David Jones referred me to an ear specialist. He informed me that he had never encountered a larger perforation. Apparently, the majority of perforated eardrums heal themselves, and I was told I could carry on as normal, but advised to keep my ear dry. So what did I do? I forgot all about that advice and a week later, when I was having a bath at home, I submerged my head in the water, as you do. Agony of agonies! That led to a sleepless, painful night. The following day I consulted Dr Jones again. The good news was, he said, that the hole was closing. It seemed likely I would escape without the need for an operation.

Victory over South Africa had been achieved at a price. Significantly, England have been drawn to meet the Springboks in a critical match at the outset of the World Cup, in Perth.

To have put over 50 points on the board against them was an amazing achievement, not least because of the way South Africa chose to play outside the laws of the game for long periods. Krige himself was shown to have been guilty of a series of misdemeanours on a video-nasty shown on Sky Sports some days afterwards. I am told the Boks returned home to South Africa in shame. That is a domestic issue, and the reality is that they have an abundance of good players. Certainly, no one in the England camp is fooled. Come the World Cup, South Africa will be a different proposition. They know there are things they must change, and they have the time to change them.

I like to think I am an honest critic of my own game. After the extraordinary start I made to my rugby union career, I think there had to be an evening-out in my performance level. No one is going to be the star in every game. Besides, I have always considered myself to be a team player. Forwards such as Richard Hill don't get enough credit for the work they do. You see Richard walking round Pennyhill Park and he is stitched here and there, on his nose, on his forehead. He may have a black eye. It's guys like that who do the real graft. When the backs have finished training, the forwards often stay out to practise scrummaging. We get some stick as we go inside, but there is mutual respect throughout the squad. In the autumn series, it was Ben Cohen and Jonny who made most headlines. Ben had a great series, and Jonny was Jonny.

I want to win games because that is what I am paid to do, by Sale and England, but the team comes before personal success. One of the reasons I don't read newspapers is that I don't want to fill my mind with things that may make me big-headed, or angry. That way is a path to a fool's paradise. I figure that what I don't identify as my weaknesses, my coaches at Sale and England will let me know. Any concerns about me being vulnerable under the high ball were quashed – not bad seeing as I'm only 5ft 8in. I will never be one of those players who are happy with second best. I wouldn't have got far with an attitude like that. If I was slothful, that is neither the person nor the image I want to project.

Unsurprisingly, the autumn series was an intense examination of our resources. The game has never been more physical than it is today. You look in a changing room after a game and it is like a casualty room. There are ice packs being distributed, big men are bruised and worn to a frazzle. Careers will be shortened, I'm in no doubt of that. No one escapes the firing line, but there seems to be a special vulnerability about young forwards in the game. I see that at Sale, young men who put themselves about on the pitch and sustain a lot of injuries. But that's the game – there is no safe way to play it. The fitter players become, the stronger and faster they make themselves, the more impact we will witness. There is no telling how much hammering a young guy starting out in the game is going to take on his body.

Look at guys coming into rucks at full speed and it is scary. If somebody in my team goes down in contact and I have to secure the ball, I am hardly the size to withstand guys from the other team flying in to clear out the ruck. At 13 stone, I have to employ the old tortoise trick – try to tuck your head out of sight before it's knocked off. There is no let-up.

A lot of players prefer to wear shoulder padding, but I'm not one of them. At Wigan, I can remember being told that if you pad up, you are protecting opponents as well as yourself. When you hit somebody and you've got pads on, the impact is going to be cushioned. If you hit them with your bony shoulder, the tackle can be more effective. Besides, I have always found padding restrictive. It's just not right for me.

What is the answer? To protect players' careers, there is an argument for restricting the number of games you play. There is only so much punishment a man's body can take in a fast, high-impact sport such as ours. I was fortunate after the autumn internationals to have been given the time by Sale's management team to let my body recover from the inevitable bumps and bruises that I collected. But, in principal, it is not easy to find a solution. Clubs pay good salaries and expect to use their best players as often as they can because they want to be successful. After Jonny Wilkinson was hurt in the match against

South Africa, for example, Newcastle slid into the relegation zone in the Zurich Premiership while he was missing. As a player, you don't want to miss any games you don't have to miss. We didn't come into the game to sit in the stand or be parked on the bench. Yet the hits taking place on the field are harder than ever before.

Rugby is played on a fine line. When you play a physical game, you expect certain things to happen, and there are incidents of foul play that will go unnoticed. As I have already said, I enjoy the physical aspect of the game – I am certainly not a prima donna – but I think there is more chance of getting away with a cheap shot in rugby union than rugby league. In league, there are only a few players in contact and it is much easier for officials to spot what is happening. In union, who can see what is going on at the bottom of a ruck or during a maul?

I get people stamping on my ankles after the ball has gone and I think, 'What am I doing here?' I can understand if every time someone gets hold of me, they want to drive me into the ground and bury me. I have no problems with that. But I do wonder about those who deal in deliberate foul play. Before I became a Christian, I was involved in the odd fight on the pitch and I have thrown a few haymakers, but no more. The game is hard enough played within the rules. I think I have the respect of most players, but don't get me wrong, they'll hit on me as hard as anybody else. I still get a good shoe-ing if I'm on the wrong side of a ruck, but most players realise I'm not there by choice.

If someone has a go at me unfairly, I recognise that their prime motivation is to put me off my game. Of what benefit would it be to the team if I was to react by punching out and getting ten minutes in the sin bin? Occasionally, I do get it wrong, and I spent ten minutes in the 'bin' against Scotland in March 2003; but mostly I keep a tight rein on my discipline, because if I rise to the bait, they have won, haven't they? Some people try to get under your skin, physically and verbally, and if they see any sign that they are succeeding, they will continue to do it. If you show them that it's not working, if they hit you after the ball you keep getting up and going back at them or keep smiling, the likelihood is the guy will get sick of his own voice. So by refusing to respond, I let them know I will not be dragged down to their level. You have to accept that's how some people play, at a base level where the laws are not as important as the result.

I know I am a target because of the way I like to play; but I also know that if somebody takes a cheap shot at me, one of the other boys will protect me. I admit that's a good feeling, knowing that you've got players around, at Sale and with England, who will look out for you. That's the good thing about a team game – people watch out for you, you're not in it on your own. I have to leave it to the officials, trust them and hope that they will punish foul play.

Marty Hulme, fitness conditioner at my club, offers a view from the touchline:

> The cheap shots will take a fine footballer out of the game if they continue. Jason is carrying quite a number of injuries, problems with his groin, problems with a knee, and that might be because of the different type of game we are playing now. Everyone is looking for Jason and marking him tight. He gets three or four guys smashing into him at a time. But it is the cheap shots that concern me.

In a European Cup game, a French player launched himself right into Jason's legs. Seriously, I thought he'd broken them. Opponents want to slow him down, I know they do. I cringe every time I see it.

In rugby league, he had played so long that opponents respected him and it was rare for anyone to take a cheap shot. But in rugby union, Jason is still the new boy on the block and there are guys wanting to take him out of the game. I have seen them try and I don't like it at all. Jason doesn't complain but it would be shameful if he was put out of the game through one cheap shot too many.

I probably give most people the benefit of the doubt, and don't apologise for that. If I let this stuff get to me and allowed the cheats to put me off my game, I would be no good to my team. I'd be lying, though, if I said it never affected me. I am not immune to what is going on and there are times when I'm pushed more than others. Most of the time it doesn't bother me, but when someone's behaviour is downright nasty, it is difficult to turn the other cheek. I think the game against South Africa was nasty.

When a team is targeting me, with sometimes three or four people on me, we have to exploit the gaps that are created elsewhere. Now that doesn't necessarily make life easier for me, but it is to the benefit of our team. For me, the constant challenge is trying to find a hole in a defence. I play on a fine line and there are times when it could go so wrong for me, so wrong for the team. But I have come this far by taking those chances and I don't feel the need to stop now. I never expected to get into the England squad as quickly as I did, and that had much to do with the fact that Dan Luger was injured. I was put on the bench and my international career took off from there. Then

I never expected to tour with the Lions, and I did, so I have walked a fine line.

That is how this game is played, on a fine line. It is perfectly legitimate to remove someone from a ruck with your boot, but, conversely, I could never think about standing on someone's ankle for the sake of it. I just try to play the way I was taught, hard but fair, and leave it at that.

I pray before I go on the pitch, not a complex prayer, or time-consuming. I just pray where I am sat. I offer a prayer of protection for the whole team. This is a sport like no other, where you are programmed to take and give punishment. If you are seen as a weak link, you will be exploited. But when the game's done, when you're physically spent, you have to be able to look the other guys in the eye and shake hands. We all play to win – but at all costs? At the cost of sportsmanship or reputation? I don't think so.

Happily, from England's perspective, the national team could hardly be in healthier condition as World Cup year 2003 began. Clive Woodward and his coaching staff have created a fantastic environment for England to move forward. He has ensured his players have the best amenities, the best support, the best scientific appraisal and most appropriate diet. All we have to do is pull on a jersey and play to the best of our ability.

14
GRAND SLAM

'The way to get the most out of victory is to follow it up with another one which makes it look small.'

HENRY S. HASKINS

Our preparations for the 2003 Six Nations Championship began for real when the squad assembled at Pennyhill Park, Bagshot, on Monday, 27 January. I was given permission to report a day late as Sale had arranged to play St Helens that night in an historic game of rugby. For the first time, two teams would play one half rugby union and one half rugby league.

I was recruited to be part of the Sale coaching staff for the occasion. We had only two sessions to teach the boys some of the fundamentals of league, but if we felt hurried in our build-up, I knew from talking to scrum-half Sean Long that St Helens were also hard pressed for time. St Helens had been to a training camp in Lanzarote to prepare for the world club challenge, and arrived home on the Friday before the scheduled match with us. Rugby union is not the kind of game that can be learned in two training sessions, either, but that was all the St Helens players had. They had brought in Gary French, son of rugby league TV commentator Ray French, to assist them. I'd played union with Gary in my days at Bath and we had a chat about the game. He was wondering how he was going to teach the St Helens boys how to scrum, ruck, maul and manage lineouts in the short period available to him. We were having a laugh – but he looked worried!

Our training went all right. Some of Sale's players go to watch rugby league, and a lot of them regularly watch the Super League on television, so they had a rough idea of what they were doing, and league is easier to pick up than union. In training, I went back over things I used to do, such as running from dummy half when we were on the attack, and it was good to have the comfort of being able to run the ball out and take the tackle and hold on to it. That takes off a lot of pressure. I play in a totally different world now; if I am isolated, there is the danger of a turnover and try time. The hardest thing for the Sale players to get accustomed to doing was retreating ten yards from the tackle area. In union you are always there on the gain line, but in league you have to retreat ten.

Part of me was really looking forward to the game, but there was a part of me that wasn't. St Helens have always been, and always will be, Wigan's fiercest rivals. Wigan fans used to tell us, if you can only win one game in a season, be certain it is against St Helens. I know their supporters were as keen to see us beaten. Lots of Wigan and St Helens fans work alongside each other, so there has always been this fierce rivalry between them. I was curious about what kind of reception I would receive as a Sale player. I should have guessed. While Apollo returned to a hero's welcome from his old club, I walked out on the pitch to a chorus of boos. St Helens fans also treated me to a song that I will not repeat here. Once a pie eater, it seems, always a pie eater. That was the name St Helens fans reserved for Wigan players.

Conditions were poor, with torrential rain and a howling wind. Even so, 12,000 people turned up for the game, making it a successful venture. That must have surprised and disappointed those who dismissed the match as a freak show. It was hard to understand why people chose to be so negative, before and afterwards, as the whole point of the game had been to raise money for both clubs by providing entertainment in a week when neither Sale nor St Helens had a fixture. Bills have to be paid, and it is useful if revenue can be generated in a blank week. It was also an opportunity to present something that had not been tried before – a game when both codes of rugby would be played on the same evening. People could see how former league players, such as Apollo and me, had adapted to union and there was a chance to see how the two codes matched up.

There was an hilarious moment in the first half – the union half – when Sale forwards were advancing up the pitch with a driving maul.

'How do you stop this?' yelled Tommy Martin, St Helens' stand-off. From the Sale side of the maul, a voice answered, 'You can't!'

We standardised the scoring system for the game, awarding five points for a try and two points for any successful kick at goal. From memory, we won the game 41–39; all our points came in the first half and all St Helens' points came in the second. I was impressed with the way all the players dealt with the game. Our boys played really well in the second half. Halfway through it we kept St Helens out for fifteen minutes. That was the key. We knew if they got a roll on, like they normally do, they'd just walk all over us. I was more or less manhandling people into position.

I was supposed to play for a certain time only, but I ended up staying on until near the end; I was enjoying it that much I didn't want to come off. I didn't score – which was probably just as well because I might not have got out with my life if I had! After the game, our boys were so proud that we had won. Although the objectives are the same, the two games are completely different. A part of me is still biased towards league – my roots, after all – but I am enjoying rugby union far more than I thought possible. No confirmation was needed that I had done the right thing by switching codes – from the moment I made my decision, I knew that I had done what was right for me – but it does mean having to think much more on the field. There are so many options, and much more pressure. Yet the style of game Sale play, and the freedom that we are allowed performing with England, has made it exciting, too. There are no rules that say we can't try to score from our own line if an opportunity exists.

After the game we had a meal with the St Helens boys, and I didn't get to bed until around midnight. I had to be up the next day at the ridiculous time of 4.15 a.m. to catch a flight from Manchester to Heathrow to join up with the England squad. It was an impossible ambition, especially as I was more tired than I supposed because I played longer than planned. Unsurprisingly, I slept in and missed my intended flight. I managed to rouse myself at 6.15 a.m. and when I got to Manchester I was further delayed because all the check-in computers at the airport had crashed.

Eventually, I made it south in time to catch the end of the day's first training session. I apologised for my late arrival and my explanation was accepted without fuss. I took full part in the second session. It was good to be back with the England squad and management. There was a lot to be taken on board, and I had to revert to the habits and mentality demanded by Clive and his staff.

This was the official start of a massive year leading to the Rugby World Cup in Australia, although no one was thinking of the World Cup as we settled down to basics at Pennyhill in late January. All that concerned us was the opening game of the Six Nations Championship against France at Twickenham. The Grand Slam had eluded us (again!) in Paris the previous spring and there was untold pressure and expectation for us to go one step further than we had before. But those were silent thoughts not voiced inside the camp, no matter the chatter that was taking place outside. Even though I rarely read newspapers or pay attention to television, I was not deaf to what was being said. In interviews before the game with France, we were constantly asked, 'Will England do the Grand Slam at last?' Many wanted to bill this first match as the Grand Slam decider. Silly, really. Hadn't Ireland beaten us to deny us a Grand Slam in 2001 and did we not have to play Ireland last in this championship, and in Dublin? Boring as it may sound, we knew all we could do was take the championship one game at a time. That was why the game with France was a big game in our minds. We could not win the Grand Slam against the French, but we sure could lose the chance of winning it if we failed against them. Our only goal was to beat France at Twickenham on 15 February.

The French had been playing really well. Like us, they'd had a good autumn series. Also, they had the confidence that springs from having won the last contest with us. We heard, too, that according to France's No. 8, Imanol Harinordoquy, England as a team were 'arrogant'. French coach Bernard Laporte was reported as saying that Will Greenwood was England's only attacking player.

As you may imagine, the management swooped on these comments and included them in the video presentation made to the England squad as the game approached. After the boys had seen the presentation, nothing was said; nothing needed to be. The message had been absorbed and, if possible, motivation stiffened.

We received one huge, desperately sad shock on the eve of the game. After dinner, we were informed that Nick Duncombe had suddenly been taken ill and died in Lanzarote. Nick was just twenty-one, in the prime of life, with a big career with Harlequins and England ahead of him. He was not only a talented scrum-half, but immensely likeable. He had been in Lanzarote to recover from injury and news of his death came out of the blue. In an instant, you realise how fragile life is. You think you have worries and problems, then you get told that Nick, so vibrant, so strong and with so much to live for, is dead and you understand that you have no reason to complain at all. It was obviously devastating for the other Quins in our squad, Jason Leonard, Will Greenwood and Dan Luger. Dan was especially close to Nick. Nick's death shook us and drew us even tighter together as a squad.

Each one of us is different on the morning of a game. Some of the boys can come down to a large breakfast and read the papers while others, including me, find it difficult to eat. I know the importance of having a decent breakfast, but if I get a couple of Weetabix down I am doing exceptionally well. Imagine the build-up to your wedding day, or the tension that is created by moving house, and you get a clue to how I feel before a big game. If you are preparing for something on the scale of an international rugby match, it has to have an effect. Dave Reddin, fitness adviser to the team, makes me a power shake with bananas, honey and other nutrients and I drink that in the late morning instead of nibbling at the pre-match meal, which is laid out at the hotel before we leave for the ground.

If you want to know who the big eaters in the squad are, you need to be around on the team night out, usually a Wednesday. There are no complaints about the kitchen at Pennyhill Park, because the food is brilliant, but it is important for us to have a change of scenery. We tend to arrive *en masse* at a nearby Italian restaurant, to be greeted with slices of pizza. You get into the habit of taking one piece after another and it is easy to eat getting on for two pizzas each before ordering. Then we have a starter, main course and dessert. Of course, there are some very big men around, but some guys get a bigger reputation than others. For instance, one of the ground rules is not to sit too close to Dorian West because those who do are likely to go home hungry.

I couldn't tell you who eats what on match days as my focus is elsewhere. Once on the team bus, someone is put in charge of the CD player. The music depends on who is the deejay; one day I recall Austin Healey bizarrely belting out songs from Wham! I have never been the deejay and have no desire to be. I tend to lose myself in my own focus.

Generally, I sit in the same seat, close to the back of the bus. Usually, Ben Kay sits next to me. A lot of the forwards seem to congregate at the back. We have a police escort and as we get nearer Twickenham the outriders part the traffic to give us priority. As we pass, people wave and cheer and you realise you are part of something special. Clive likes to have the team at the ground around one hour and forty minutes before the kick-off. As we leave the bus, supporters shout their encouragement. Already there is a buzz in the air that gives you a lift. You know that so many people are behind you.

Pinned to a wall in the dressing room is a timetable for the afternoon. We know precisely when we have to be out for the introductions on the pitch and the anthems. Before then, players go out in their own time for a warm-up and look around the stadium. Jonny Wilkinson is out early to practise kicking and to gauge the wind direction. I do likewise.

All the real work is behind us. It is hard to appreciate the amount of data and information that Clive and his staff place at our disposal. We have videos and CDs with a complete break-down on our opponents, all logged individually. We know a player's preferred angle of running, we know who kicks off which foot, where they like to kick and how they position them-selves to receive kicks. Those who need to know will have concise reports on the opposition's scrummaging and lineout plays.

Prior to game day, I look at the players I will be up against, concentrating on the back three. I want to know all their pref-erences so I can exploit what areas of weakness I identify. Against France, that meant getting to know Clement Pointrenaud, Aurelien Rougerie and Vincent Clerc. One fact I learned was that these are three seriously quick men.

Like I said, we operate these days in a no-excuse zone. We are looked after and treated in the most professional manner. If you have happy players, of course, you tend to have a successful team. That is what Clive is creating.

The honour of leading England out against France fell to Jason Leonard, who was winning his one hundredth cap for his country. Jason has been in the squad for a dozen years, a remarkable achievement. His record is more phenomenal when you consider that he has bridged the old, six-pints-a-night ethos of the amateur era to be influential in this age of ultra-professionalism. Jason has told a few tales of how it used to be, but he has adapted, survived and flourished in today's game. The days when forwards could just trundle from one scrum to the next are long over. In training nowadays, Jason does drills involving spinning off defenders or side-stepping them. It's not that you want your front rows to do too much of that stuff, but we want England forwards to be able to go in at first man and pass the ball off.

The closest the backs get to scrummaging is to stand on the scrum-machine at training to provide some weight for the forwards to shove against. That's how it should be. Backs job description: score. Forwards job description: bash each other. It's as simple as that.

They've got the rough end of the stick, but then for some there is no choice. How many youngsters do you think are running around parks dreaming of being a prop-forward for England? You get to a certain age, look at your shape, and know you have an automatic position, but to opt to play in the front row is to accept a position where hard and largely unseen work is far removed from the glamour side of the game. I am the first to acknowledge that forwards do not get enough praise.

Jason is the first forward to make a 'ton' – as he would say in his thick London accent – and we were all delighted for him to be given an ovation as he made it on to the pitch alone. He's a team player, great family man and a genuinely nice guy.

In Paris the previous season, one tactic that turned up trumps for the French was to set flanker Serge Betsen on to Jonny like a terrier. Betsen closed Jonny down. For Twickenham, Clive had his own surprise for the French; he chose my Sale team-mate Charlie Hodgson in the centre. Like Jonny, Charlie is a stand-off at club level. While the decision was greeted with much scepticism – Charlie had never played in the centre before – Clive reasoned that his selection would be beneficial on two levels. Charlie would be a foil for Jonny, giving us the option of going to either of them in attack; and Charlie's presence would dilute France's defence because they would not have an obvious target in Jonny alone. I know how good a kicker Charlie is, and how he can break down defences. It would not be as simple for the French to close Jonny and Charlie down. Betsen is a good player, but he was almost non-existent on the day and never came close to disrupting Jonny as he had in Paris. Just after an hour, Betsen was withdrawn, clearly an indication that the balance of the tactical battle had swung in England's favour.

My first touch of the ball in the match was collecting a French kick to touch and throwing to myself. From there, I managed to beat the first man. Confidence-wise, this is important to me. To be honest, fear of being caught spurs me on to beat first man. When I do, that's worth three points in the psychology stakes. It is always good to get an early run, it lifts the crowd and your team; my confidence rises and I have put doubt in the minds of the other team. If they change tactics and opt to kick shorter so I can't get a quick throw, they haven't gained as much yardage.

Jason's game came to a premature end when he left the field in the first half with a hamstring injury. We all knew that he would be back to fight another day.

At half-time we led 12–7 thanks to Jonny's boot. One of our strengths is that if opponents illegally slow the ball down or put a hand on the ball on the ground, we get the penalty and that is invariably three points. Either they can let us have the ball and then we are able to play as fast as we like; or they spoil the game, we get the penalty and hurt them nearly every time. Jonny is that good and that consistent.

Fair play to him, the hours and hours he spends training is to our benefit on match days. When everyone else has gone in, he will be out on the pitch kicking balls. If he had a penny for every kick he has made, he could stop playing already. The best way I can put it is to say I am so glad he is on our team and England doesn't have to play against him.

We don't take his kicking for granted, but we know he won't miss many. We don't set out to win matches by penalties, yet when push comes to shove, Jonny is Mister Reliable. Is there pressure on him? You bet there is. It's a job I wouldn't like to do. Yet Jonny can kick off both feet – incredible, really. I have never seen anyone like him. To comprehend how goal-kicking responsibility can destroy a man, France's Gerald Merceron missed five penalties in the match. He was sacked for France's next game.

France scored the only try of the first half when Olivier

Magne charged down a kick from Charlie, caught the high bouncing ball and sailed over the line. The French habitually punish mistakes. If your ball is turned over, they can be lethal as they counter-attack from anywhere on the field.

I scored a try in the first quarter of the second half that allowed us to draw into a lead that would always be challenging for the French. The forwards did some strong, surging work on the right side of the pitch, sucking a lot of Frenchmen in. I was hovering in the middle of the field between two of their defenders. The ball was moved left to Will Greenwood. I picked my line, one of their players rushed up and Will threw a long, perfect pass over the top. I caught the ball and darted between the posts unhindered. One of my objectives before the game was to try to find holes to run in, or to find mismatches against forwards. When something like that opens up, you have to make sure that you take it. The feeling of elation that accompanies placing the ball down is something that never goes away.

That try gave us some breathing space, but for the last minutes of the game we stopped playing. We kicked the ball away too much. We gave France the ball they wanted and they punished us for it. They scored two more tries, through Pointrenaud and Damien Traille, and we were grateful that Jonny had already taken his personal score to 20 points. At the end, we were happy we had achieved our objective of winning the match, but we were disappointed with conceding those tries in a 25–17 victory. They had scored three to our one; defensively, that was unacceptable to us as a team. After the game, people were saying what if Merceron had kicked his goals, but you can't live off 'what ifs'. He didn't and that's how it goes.

If we were disgruntled with the way we had played, we took

heart from knowing there was so much room for improvement. Our goal had been to win the game and it did not matter to us if it was by 1 point or by 100 points. In the dressing room after the match, Clive and Martin Johnson usually say something, and this time their message was similar: well done, we won, but let's be honest, we can and must improve.

That evening there was a black-tie dinner at a central London hotel. I understand it is part of the tradition, but as a player I have to say it would be better to be back at the team hotel with my feet up. At least Amanda was able to come to the dinner. Her parents had come down to London with her and the children and were kind enough to baby-sit for the evening.

I like to have my family around at all times. The children miss me, Amanda misses me and I miss them. So wherever I go, my family goes. The importance of this was something I stressed when I made the switch to rugby union. I knew that if I was to be involved with England, there would be a lot of time away and what I didn't want to do was affect my family. Looking back on the autumn series when Amanda couldn't come down because of our new baby, that was a hard time for us. I think I perform better when my family is there than when they are not. In retrospect, by my standards I had a quieter autumn series. I know it doesn't work for everybody to have their family around their workplace. We can do it because we school our children at home and because Amanda, as their teacher, does not go out to work. Clive has happily accommodated me.

If England's management wants me to be the best I can be on match days, this is the arrangement that I believe makes me play my best. There's nothing worse than being away at camp and having other matters playing on your mind. With the children around, I can see them before they go to bed, even if it is sometimes for only half an hour or an hour. I've got to make sure that I look after myself and Amanda is aware that there are times when I am in the zone – rugby robot.

At the hotel, I have a separate room but by popping in and out I try to make it as normal as possible for us all. On our days off, many of the players are able to go home to see their families, but that's not practical for us. So my family make their home at Pennyhill Park and the staff is great with them. We're happy, and that makes it easier for me to perform to the best of my ability on the field.

People expect you to play at a certain level week in week out, and that requires a lot of preparation. While I am studying the opponents I am to meet, other teams are going through the stats and looking closely at my game. It's like a game of chess. You try to stay one step ahead. I am not a worrier. I am self-confident in what I do and I'll back myself. As I have said, I don't claim to be the smartest, the fastest or the best in the world. I just want to be the best I can be. I know what sort of game I have had. I can come off the field after scoring a couple of tries and know that I have had an average game, yet in the papers I will be made out to be a star. At the other end of the scale, there will be a game where I have really worked hard, covered the pitch from one side to the other, not had much of the ball and not got close to scoring, yet I'll end the match believing I've done my job. Some days you have to contend with taking a few balls up the middle and working twice as hard in defence.

On the Monday following the French game, we began to

prepare for Wales. They were a team under immense pressure after losing the first game of the championship to Italy. Welsh rugby is not having the best of times. Yet our instinct told us that after losing that game, the Welsh players were hurting and the pain would only go away if they responded with a better performance against England. Wales' defeat in Rome was going to make our work harder. I'd rather play a team that has had an easy win the week before.

In the media's view, again made clear to me from interviews we gave, the result was a foregone conclusion. England were coming to town to steamroller the Welsh, they said. Obviously, we are a lot smarter than to have a blind belief in that kind of rhetoric. We knew we were going into the lion's den, so to speak. If Wales could beat England, to a man they would become national heroes overnight. It seems that in the Six Nations Championship every team has England in their sights. We are the benchmark at this time.

I had never played against Wales in rugby union; in 2001 I was in the A-team when England met the Welsh, and in 2002 I missed the game through injury. My first impression of the Millennium Stadium could be summed up in one word: amazing. On the eve of a match, we like to look at the ground where we are to play the next day so as to know what to expect. In Cardiff, the crowd is close to the touchline, right on top of you. I was really looking forward to the experience of playing there. I've played in a lot of big stadiums – Wembley, Twickenham, the Olympic Stadium in Sydney – and I am not troubled by a noisy crowd. Noise is only against you if you want it to be. Once you hear a roar, it's a roar. I like to think I can use the atmosphere to motivate me.

Wales had already scrapped their A-team, another clear signal that the game is in transition there. One of the keys to England's success is having young players coming through in the A-team squad. We train as a squad of fifty players until it's game time, which enables young men such as James Simpson-Daniel, Phil Christophers and Josh Lewsey to slide more easily into the England team than they might otherwise do when the call comes. This is invaluable to the team. I wonder how younger players in Wales are getting international experience.

I was looking forward to catching up with Iestyn Harris, who had been playing rugby league for Leeds during my latter days at Wigan but was now in the Welsh union set-up. He had always said he wanted to play for Wales at rugby union. Probably what appealed to him about union appealed to me, with both of us looking further afield to the World Cup. In a way, I feel sorry for Iestyn because I've seen how hard it has been for him to make his mark in Wales. Having played against him, I am aware of the skills he has and I know how dangerous a player he can be. His misfortune was to come into a struggling team, and with the Welsh public demanding change, Iestyn was thrown into the team at No. 10 and labelled the nation's saviour. That was a huge weight around his neck, leaving him with a very hard job in the international arena. I am so glad that I was introduced into the England team gently, given twenty minutes here, another fifteen to twenty minutes there. I was also coming into a team brimming with confidence; it was easier for me to adapt. Once his honeymoon with the Welsh public was over, Iestyn was subjected to a great deal of criticism. He was on the bench against England. In a sense, he is a wasted talent.

England made two changes for the Welsh game: Graham

Rowntree replaced Jason in the front row and Kyran Bracken was chosen at scrum-half ahead of Andy Gomarsall. For a while, Wales gave us a real run for our money.

For me, it was very disappointing to take a heavy knock inside the first five minutes. I took on a high bomb. A full-back normally goes for everything struck in the air, but as I was chasing the ball I realised I wasn't going to get it. I don't think it was kicked properly. As I ran, a Welsh player just clipped me with his leg below my right knee. There was no malice, but I knew it was a massive bang around my tibia and fibula. The pain got worse and worse and I couldn't walk properly let alone run. The odd few times I did get the ball I was in a lot of discomfort. You always hope that you will be able to run something off, but my leg was tightening and the pain was being transferred all the way to my calf. I told the medical staff to keep a close eye on me because I was struggling.

Just before half-time I knew I was fighting a losing battle. I delivered another message to the medical team – 'You've got to get me off.' I felt a liability. At times you can stay on, as I had done when I took that kick to my head in the game with South Africa in the previous autumn, but this time the soreness in my leg was getting worse, not better. I knew I had to leave the game, but before I had a chance to do so, Wales launched an attack down our right flank through Mark Taylor. I was hoping this wouldn't happen. I had Taylor coming towards me and he had support from two swift team-mates. I had time to see that Ben Cohen was chasing Taylor from behind, so it was crucial that I held up the Welshman for as long as possible to let Ben get to him. Just hold Taylor, I urged myself.

Had he given the pass early, Wales' full-back would have

drawn me, then passed the ball out to the winger and England's defences would have been naked. All I was hoping was that I could gain some time for Ben. How? Years of experience, I think. You make it look as though, if he passes, you have got the outside man covered. You are luring him into running a bit further. As he is weighing his options, he is not running flat out and what he doesn't realise is that we have men tracking him back at full pace. When it got to the stage of making a decision, I turned blind to him. Had Taylor passed then, I am quite sure they'd have scored. But I had tempted him to going on his own, allowing Ben to arrive at pace. We both flung our bodies at him and Wales' chance was lost.

Had they scored just before half-time, they would have been back into the game and really confident. It was a close call. It is imperative that if you are injured you disguise the fact from the opposition or they will pick you out. But with this last-ditch run the game was up for me. Miserably, I headed for the dressing room. I can probably count on one hand the times when I have left the pitch through injury. It was disappointing because, mentally, I was set for a big game. I was still feeling low when the rest of the guys came in for the break. Players were being patched up, taking drinks and readying themselves for the second half. It is easy to feel out of it.

I watched the second half from the sidelines, but I admit I was probably in a bit of a sulk. I had pain behind my knee, like a pulling sensation, all the way down to my foot. England won 26–9, but again there was a sense that the team had not found top gear. I was one of the walking injured excused attending the dinner that night, but I still didn't manage to get to sleep before 4 a.m.

The next day, back at Pennyhill Park, it was clear I was struggling and it was arranged for me to return home for a scan on Tuesday. Fortunately, Sale was without a game the following weekend so it meant I would not miss any action with my club. The scan showed no serious damage to my knee and I was able to lift some weights and ride an exercise bike to maintain my overall fitness. I was working hard and felt I was making decent progress in my race to be fit to play for England against Italy, but there is a distinct difference between feeling fit and being fit to do the work on the pitch.

I kept in contact with the England medical team, and with Clive, and I felt guardedly optimistic that I could take the field against Italy, fifteen days after I had been injured. On the Monday of game week, I spoke to England doctor Simon Kemp, and to Clive, and the decision was taken to travel south. Amanda and the children were in the car with me when there was a change of heart. Clive came to the conclusion that it was unwise to take a risk with me against the Italians. So, after this latest phone call, I turned the car round and drove the family home. We had gone about twenty miles, so this was no big deal. After leaving Amanda and the kids, I set off once more to join the squad. It is usual for all the players to report to Pennyhill at least for a couple of days. Those not fit, or selected, then go home. I did have a light training session on the pitch and the following day I was sore. It would have been senseless to push my knee further, especially as bigger games with Scotland and Ireland were over the horizon.

My absence provided Josh Lewsey from Wasps with an opportunity to come into the team as full-back. Naturally, I wished him all the best. Josh had been waiting in the wings and we knew the talent he had. Healthy competition is an important ingredient in the England squad.

Charlie Hodgson was dropped to the bench as Mike Tindall came back into the team. Charlie must have thought he had been presented with an ideal chance to showcase his ability when Jonny took a knock after half-time and was taken out of the game for his own protection. Summoned as Jonny's replacement, Charlie was given the opportunity to play at his preferred position of No. 10. Unfortunately for him, he had barely warmed up before he collapsed to the ground in distress. The injury was to prove serious. He had damaged medial ligaments in a knee, and his chances of being selected for the World Cup suddenly looked very remote.

He has the sympathy of the entire England squad. I sent him a text message, encouraging him to keep his chin up. I am not sure how I would have reacted to being injured with the World Cup beckoning. To his enormous credit, Charlie has stayed positive.

I had planned to watch the Italy game at home, but as I was going to a meeting of our house fellowship group in Warrington, I made arrangements for someone to video the match in case I wasn't back in time. I ended up staying with the group longer than I anticipated – it was an exceptionally good meeting – so I missed the first twenty-two minutes when England were on fire, scoring five tries. Of course, I saw it later and watched in admiration as Josh took his two tries in a sure-footed performance. England won 40–5. If England did not maintain the tempo at which they started the game, that was due to the Italians' big-hearted effort and the fact that it is hard to remain mentally switched on when the match is obviously won.

Unsurprisingly, Josh's performance caught the eye of the media. Some reporters asked him if he would expect to keep me out of the team to play Scotland. Now no one has a right to an England shirt, but it was astonishing that after just one game it was convenient to forget the impact I had made over a period of some time. Some were quick off the mark to write me off. I am told that's newspapers for you! Josh and I had a laugh over what was being said and written. Without wishing to sound arrogant, I felt that my contribution to the team up until then was enough to keep me in the side. Out of courtesy, Clive and I spoke in the countdown to the next game, against Scotland, and neither of us was bothered by what was being debated. Clive said, as he always says, that he wanted the best team he could pick on the pitch.

Before England's game with Scotland, I had the chance to prove my fitness by playing for Sale in their Zurich Premiership match at Leeds. Every game at this level is a big one, and I was determined not to miss another club game. Sale coach Jim Mallinder let me have as much time as I needed before he picked the team. In my mind, I was always going to play, but it was only a couple of days before the game that I realised I could play with confidence. I still had some pain – but who has ever played 100 per cent fit? I always enjoyed playing against my home-town club.

On the day, I scored two tries and experienced no after effects. For the second one, centre Graeme Bond off-loaded the ball to me and I weaved my way in and out of the Leeds defence and managed to get to the line. It was a good return, thankfully. Even so, there were those still questioning whether I would get the England shirt back.

No doubt Clive was pleased that Josh had forced his way into the picture. Every coach likes to have options when it comes to selection, and Clive is no different. Players shouldn't get picked on reputation and name alone although sometimes it makes sense for a coach to go with a player whom he knows has performed when it mattered. You get a name in the game – in any game for that matter – only if you have done the business over a period of time, but players respect a coach who picks his team on merit. It is a strong motivation for those in the team and for those trying to get into the side. It is reassuring to know that the door is open.

In the event, when Clive unveiled the England team at Pennyhill Park on the Monday before the Scotland game, he had elected to play me on the wing, leaving Josh at full-back. I was happy with that. I had played on the wing for almost ten seasons, moving to full-back for the previous eighteen months. If I was asked what is my favourite position, I'd probably say full-back, but a move to the wing was not a big deal. I had no axe to grind. The main thing was that we had our strongest team out, which is how it should be. Clive wants to have a versatile England back line. We can go anywhere we like on the field to get our hands on the ball. He wants strike players who can strike from anywhere. With that luxury, he can put doubts into the minds of other teams. Going to the wing required a bit of an adjustment, of course. I had to run moves from a different angle. I was also told that I'd be cover for centre, and that meant a lot of homework.

England versus Scotland is always a huge occasion, at any sport. We were short-priced favourites, but that was going to count for little unless we matched the Scots for commitment and passion from the first whistle to the last. Even so, I never supposed for a second that my own commitment would result in ten minutes in the sin-bin. It was laughable, really it was. Two Scotland players, Andrew Mower and Simon Taylor, were sin-binned within two minutes of each other for offences against Mike Tindall and Josh, respectively. That set the scene and I presumed that the first England player to commit any kind of misdemeanour would be in trouble. That somebody just happened to be me.

But what was my offence? I don't know to this day. Scotland winger Kenny Logan had the ball and I shaped to tackle him. He sensed this and, probably a step and half before I went to tackle him, he kicked ahead. Kenny then ran into me and did what looked a great dive. What do you do if you are going in to tackle somebody and they kick the ball at the last moment? Do I suddenly make myself invisible? I could understand I deserved punishment if I went in with my shoulder, but I did not. I just couldn't get out of his way and Kenny took advantage of the situation. I saw him after the game and said ten out of ten for the dive, and he smiled.

I got the yellow card because the referee said I was obstructing Kenny and had to go. I felt like I was made the scapegoat – sent to the bin to even the sides up a little. I didn't deliberately obstruct Kenny. It was a bit like when someone takes a dive in the penalty area in football when they haven't been touched. I hope we don't end up with regular incidents like this. It was embarrassing to go off because of such a bad decision.

It was not the first time, either. Earlier in the season I was victim of another ludicrous decision when Sale played Bourgoin in the Heineken Cup. When the ball was charged down in our defensive third of the pitch, I was involved in a race with a prop from the French club. We touched shoulder to shoulder – perfectly legitimate – but then he wanted to wrestle. I ended up getting his arm and pulling him back because what he was doing was so blatant, or so I thought. I mean, why would I need to get into a shirt-tugging contest with a prop in a foot race over twenty yards? But, again, I placed too much faith in the official. The referee sent me to the sin-bin because, he said, 'You pulled him back twice.' I had only one response: 'You're kidding, aren't you?' He wasn't, and I had ten minutes in the sin-bin.

At Twickenham, I sat at the side of the pitch itching to get back into the game. It's strange when you find you want to redeem yourself for a crime that you have not committed. At least Josh scored while I was out of the game, so no ground was lost in my absence.

As events unravelled, I was asked to switch from the wing to centre in the second half when Mike Tindall came off. I was relieved I had done the homework necessary to slot into that position, and two opportunities came my way when I happened to be in the right place at the right time. The Scots began to get a little loose, especially round the fringes, and I took advantage of a tapped penalty by Matt Dawson. I saw a hole in the Scots defence and, gathering a pass from Daws, managed to beat full-back Glenn Metcalfe on the outside. In the last ten minutes, when Daws made another sniping run, I tried to get as close to the ball as possible. He managed to ride a tackle and slip the ball to me, and I made the final metres over the line. England claimed victory, 40–9.

Even with a couple of tries, I didn't leave the ground thinking I had had one of my better games. In truth, I spent too much of the match chasing the ball. Some days are like that, so you just learn the lessons and move on.

Only Ireland remained, with hardly any gap between the games. Now – and only now – we began to talk about the Grand Slam. We had a belief in the squad that no matter the failures that had gone before, we would not miss out on the prize this time. We were resolved to complete a mission that for most us was considered unfinished business.

However, the Irish were chasing the same goal. England may not have won a Grand Slam since 1995, but for the Irish the wait had been somewhat longer, since 1948. Having denied England the Slam in October 2001, we suspected the Irish would be rubbing their hands with glee at the prospect of not only stopping us again, but with the added incentive of taking the Grand Slam themselves. There could be no more fitting finale to the last Six Nations match before the 2003 World Cup.

I had a family interlude during the immediate aftermath of the Scotland game as Jemimah celebrated her third birthday on Tuesday, 25 March. We had brought her presents with us so that she could open them at the hotel. Jemimah already loves clothes and shoes; clearly, she is going to be an ideal shopping partner for her mum. She loves the colour pink.

The day before – a day off for the squad – we had been to a farm not too far from the hotel, and Jemimah had stroked lambs and piglets. It was an ideal family outing although I'm not necessarily the best company for forty-eight hours after a game. I find it takes me a couple of days to recover physically from a match. I did try my best to be enthusiastic as we roamed

Odds Farm, but I cannot vouch for how well I succeeded. Anyway, I don't think Jemimah was too troubled if Daddy was a little preoccupied. In her little world, she had love, presents and, for her birthday tea, a cake with candles. The staff at Pennyhill can never do enough for us, and Cameron and Jemimah have come to know lots of them by name. Certainly, her birthday seemed to offer Jemimah enough excitement.

Our task in the England squad was to contain our excitement and focus on the job before us. After all, this was one of the biggest weeks in any of our careers. We had fallen down in Dublin the last time – the Irish put us under pressure and we never replied – and so we were more determined than ever to beat them in their own backyard. This added up to a media and marketing man's dream. The game dominated all rugby talk, and we knew from the moment we arrived in Dublin on Thursday afternoon that Irish anticipation was close to hysterical.

All the nitty-gritty of our preparation had been done at Pennyhill Park, and we were given Friday off. As Amanda, her parents and the children were not arriving on the ferry from Liverpool until the next day, I made a point of scheduling a programme of total relaxation. I got up later than usual and sauntered down to the hotel's health club. I bumped into hooker Dorian West as I was making arrangements with one of the girls at reception. Dorian couldn't believe what I was doing. 'Jason Robinson, one of the toughest wingers in the world, is booking a facial,' he spluttered. Ever since I can remember I have suffered from ingrown hairs on my face, so once a year I treat myself to a facial. This was the day I was pampering myself. Afterwards, I felt totally relaxed.

The game was due to be played on Sunday afternoon, so the following morning we had training. It was really a matter of rehearsing all that we had put in place.

After lunch I took Cameron out to buy some cards for Amanda for Mother's Day, and around the city there was a noticeable buzz. I was approached several times and everyone was complimentary. Not unnaturally, people let me know that they wanted Ireland to win, but all of them politely wished me luck for the next day. Once in town, Cameron kindly told me that their nan had already sorted out their cards. Still, I bought my card and Cameron got something for his mum. I thought it would be good for us to have the rest of the afternoon together. I am aware that one of the drawbacks of my life as a professional sportsman is that everything has to revolve around me. Everyone has to fit in with my training, my rest, my matches. It's good when, at least occasionally, something can happen on their terms. The Four Seasons Hotel had already made a big impression on Cameron and Jemimah when they found cakes waiting for them on plates decorated with their names. It was a lovely personal touch.

After finishing at the shops, Cameron and I went to the hotel swimming pool – the water was not too deep, so there was no need to worry if the lifeguards were on duty for me! I let Cameron try the sauna and the steam room as he had never been in those before. He was chuffed. Finally, we had a couple of milkshakes before Cameron joined Amanda and the others. It was a relief to be able to take my mind off the game for a few hours.

I joined the other players for a 6 p.m. team meeting. When the coaches had finished their briefings and gone through the basics, there was a video presentation to finish with, as usual. The film showed clips of England's most dramatic moments in the championship, our tries and big tackles, run against a soundtrack of high-tempo music. The theme of the film was that our moment had arrived and phrases including 'One opportunity' and 'One chance' were flashed on the screen. I don't know how the others felt, but I went to bed that evening feeling a responsibility not to let anyone down. Sleep did not come too easily, I can tell you.

Next morning we had our usual match-day get-together to ensure everyone was fit to play. I could feel an edginess like never before in the team room. I am not normally as agitated as I was. There were a lot of nervous men, but I could sense that everyone was ready for what lay ahead of us. I just *knew* this was going to be England's day. In his final address before we left the hotel for the ground, Clive told us, 'Many people are going to wish you good luck today. Just say to them, "We don't need good luck because we are good enough to win without relying on luck."' Clive just wanted us to play the game the way he knew we could.

At Lansdowne Road, the dressing room that was festooned in England flags and familiar banners. The intention was to make us feel as much at home as possible. One poster reminded us that we were here to win, and nothing else mattered. I'd been here before and one of the characteristics of the place is that when a train passes it feels like it is going over the changing room. You feel the room shudder. On this day, the whole place was shaking in expectation of the game anyway. Our timetable was pinned to a wall as usual, and we knew precisely the moment we were supposed to be on the pitch for the pre-match ceremonies. We left at the appointed time and lined up on the side of the pitch we were defending in the first half. We could never have guessed the shenanigans that were to follow.

As we stood in a line, all I could hear was part of the crowd booing. I had no clue why this was happening. We were charged up, focused on the game. Eventually, we were told that Ireland's president, Mary McAleese, was not coming on to the pitch to be introduced to the teams until the England team had moved to the other side of the red carpet. In all the noise, I heard an English voice reply, 'It's going to be a long day then.' I have no idea who it was who spoke, but the sentiment had full backing from the team. This was a massive Grand Slam decider and we didn't want to be caught up in what was developing into an international incident. Donal Lenihan, who was part of the Lions management team in Australia in 2001 and a man I liked, was one of those who took exception to England's unwillingness to shift. That was a disappointment. Donal should understand that players are in a zone of their own just before kick-off.

The protocol that was expected on the day should have been made plain beforehand, and not after we had taken our position. Why weren't we told that we were expected to line up on the other side of the halfway line? We did not know it was traditional for Ireland to line up where we were standing. That was the cause of all the confusion. We did not act arrogantly; in fact, I'd argue that there is not an ounce of arrogance in this England squad. Eventually, the Irish boys went round the other side so that they could stand on the left of England. After a lot of huffing and puffing – and with so much riding on the result that any little moment was blown out of proportion – the presentation party proceeded to greet us. I am sorry if the Irish president got her shoes dirty; the misunderstanding meant that she had to walk on part of the pitch not covered with a red carpet.

Once the game kicked off, the noise was deafening. David Humphreys kicked Ireland ahead with a dropped goal and the decibel level went higher still. Humphreys is a man with a good boot, so we had to nullify the danger he represented. Defence was the key to our victory. We wanted the game played on our terms and if that meant keeping the ball tight that was what we would do.

Martin Johnson and the forwards set England's platform – not that I want to know much about driving mauls, but it raised the spirit when I watched Jonno and the boys shift the Irish forwards back five, ten, fifteen yards. If the forwards don't go forward, you play the game on the back foot. England's commitment was total, the ferocity of the forwards' work breath-taking. Our job in the back line was to support them all we could, seize attacking moments and breach any holes that appeared. With a strong wind against us, it was immensely pleasing to restrict Ireland's attacking opportunities to next to nothing. Even so, at one point the scoreboard read Ireland 6 England 7. After Lawrence Dallaglio had punished the Irish with a try from a cleverly worked move from the base of an attacking scrum – Jonny flicked over the conversion, of course – Humphreys claimed a penalty to bring the scores to within one point.

The Irish supporters could never have imagined that those were the last points their team would score. When there is slow ball and nothing on, how valuable it is for a team to have a man like Jonny who can drop into the pocket and keep the scoreboard ticking over. Before half-time, he slotted two dropped goals with his weaker right foot. But Jonny's Jonny; you half suspect he could back heel them over. At half-time it was Ireland 6 England 13.

Our game was tactically sound. The Irish players, including Brian O'Driscoll who had been superb in other matches, were not getting time, space or, crucially, the ball. Our forwards' work rate and the intensity of their play simply overwhelmed Ireland. We struck again with a second try when Mike Tindall scored by the posts after a finely judged, angled run. With Jonny temporarily off the field for treatment to a cut in his mouth, substitute Paul Grayson converted the try.

Will Greenwood scored the first of his two tries when he gathered the ball close to the Irish line. Will swore afterwards that pure strength had enabled him to get to the line – and he was right. He simply forgot to add that it was the strength of half the England pack that hustled him through the stretched Irish defence!

By this point, the silence in Lansdowne Road was deafening. Ireland's loud and proud supporters could sense this was England's hour and no amount of shouting was going to stop us. For our part, we were urging one another to retain concentration and not to weaken for a second. 'No tries, no tries,' was the battle call as we determined to deny Ireland the slightest consolation. Even though in command, I was not alone in wondering how much longer it could go on. All over the pitch, big, strong men were feeling pain. But when you are leading, you console yourself with the knowledge that no matter how tired you are feeling, the other team is feeling far worse. Our resolve never crumbled.

Will's second try started when I squared up to tackle Geordan Murphy deep in Irish territory. Geordan flicked the ball back inside, straight into Will's arms. Will ran to the corner flag and placed the ball down. I can imagine Jonny thinking, 'Well, thanks, Will.' The conversion was unimportant, of course; and England's other try from substitute Dan Luger was popped over by Jonny. The scoreboard told the story: Ireland 6 England 42.

When the final whistle blew, I felt a great relief. All the pressure that had built up in the previous days was released. Had we lost that game who knows what damage might have been done to morale. We had not dared contemplate the consequences of not winning, not through arrogance, but through a sense of narrow-eyed determination not to come up one game short again.

The disappointment of the Irish players was plain to all, but there was no shame in their defeat and they can move towards the World Cup with optimism of their own. I swapped shirts with Denis Hickie. This time, unlike the last occasion in 2001, when we were called forward to collect our medals, we went to receive them as winners, not losers. The questions that had surrounded England prior to the game had now been answered. Could England win a big match when the Grand Slam was at stake? Yes, we could. Could England win away from 'fortress' Twickenham when it mattered? Yes, we could. We had removed the monkey from our backs.

All those hours of work, all the sweat and spilled blood had been worthwhile. All the sacrifices we make as professional sportsmen, the long periods away from home, seem worthwhile when you fulfil what you set out to achieve. But all this takes time to sink in, and that night at the official dinner I felt a little low. I had to have some caffeine to perk up.

Once upon a time, the bigger the game, the more I drank afterwards. Those days are long gone, but on this occasion I did take a glass of champagne with Amanda. During the evening I also caught up with Brian O'Driscoll and Rog – Ronan O'Gara – who were team-mates on the Lions tour. It was good to find out how their lives are going outside of rugby.

So, the Grand Slam belonged to England and as a team we owe a debt of gratitude to Clive, his coaching staff and the medical boys. I am proud to be associated with a group of special players and management. They tell me this is an achievement we will share as a group for the rest of our lives.

I had achieved so much in rugby league that it is hard to comprehend this level of success in rugby union. After a mere eighteen caps, I found myself part of England's first Grand Slam for eight years. I have scored eleven tries for England and finished the Lions tour as top try scorer. I consider myself blessed and anticipate the future with excitement.

I have paid a small price for my success. There is a saying that your teeth are not your own until you have retired from the game. In my case, it's my nose and fingers that have taken most punishment. I can't breathe properly out of my right nostril – the cartilage has moved – and two fingers on my right hand don't function as they should. That hand is like a claw. I will have the necessary surgery when I'm done with a rugby ball.

I consider it my great good fortune to have switched codes at a time when there are so many good English players around, beginning with Martin Johnson. He's an imposing man to have as captain. At 5ft 8in, I stand next to him and feel like I should be calling him Dad. Jonno leads by example. He never takes a backward step and you know that when the heat is on he will be there. Not only is he a great leader, he is a great player, too.

There are leaders all across the team. Lawrence Dallaglio lost his place as first choice in the back row and worked himself into the ground to get back into contention. He is world class and a man who can take decisions. Richard Hill and Neil Back continually put their bodies on the line for England. After a game I see them battered, often with a black eye and a face stitched back together; but a week later, there they are again. Daws – Matt Dawson – bosses the forwards and gets them on the move from scrum-half. All good No. 9s need a bit of mongrel in them and that's Daws – a mongrel with a bone. He's feisty, a bit cocky, and if things are not happening he will let the forwards know. He is their eyes.

Sometimes Will Greenwood just plods about the place. He is laid back to the point of falling over. He is known as 'Shaggy' after the character from Scooby-Doo. To look at him, you would not think that he is a world-class centre, but on match day he is totally switched on; he is one of those players who makes things happen out of nothing. Tins – Mike Tindall – reclaimed his place as Will's partner in the centre after losing his position through injury and a loss of form. His club, Bath, had a poor season, but credit to Tins, he fought his way back. He's a down-to-earth lad.

I have a laugh with Graham Rowntree, Dorian West and Trevor Woodman from the front row. Once I seven-balled Trevor at pool – that is I potted all my balls before he had knocked in one – and whenever I see him I just smile. He knows why.

By definition, a team is a group brought together from different backgrounds, with different characteristics. But a team becomes a team when everyone is united in a common cause.

That's England 2003. I feel like twenty or so brothers surround me. We are in this together. I suppose because rugby is a physical game, it brings us closer still. We watch out for each other. That weekend in Dublin, I knew I was part of something special.

15
FAMILY MATTERS

'The most important thing a father can do for his children is to love their mother.'

THEODORE HESBURGH

Never in my wildest dreams as a ten year old in Leeds did I think that I would become an international in rugby league and rugby union.

I played rugby because it brought me pleasure. On a rugby pitch, I could be myself in a way I never could in a classroom. I had an identity. In school I was timid and shy, but when I was given a ball I changed into a different kid. I ran and, more often than not, I could not be caught. This gift led to a game I loved becoming my job; and a job that has transformed my whole lifestyle.

Yet this has not been achieved without cost. I have tried to be open about my mistakes, but some things are apparent only to those closest to me.

My family is more interested in me being a loving husband and father, not some superstar with his head in the clouds. Do not misunderstand me. I really enjoy playing rugby, but there is a reality to my life that extends beyond the freeze-frame moment on the pitch. Moments such as scoring a try down the left-hand side of the field for the British Lions against Australia in 2001 are the pinnacle. People don't see the hard work and all the other sacrifices you have to make. It's not easy for Amanda at times, or for the wife of any professional sportsman. They are the ones who bear the brunt of a bad performance or a poor run of form. I am thankful Amanda is not obsessed with rugby. The last thing you need when you get home is another coach! When I get home from a game, she is usually none the wiser. She will ask, 'Did you play? Did you score?' and that's kind of it. That suits me.

Our son Joseph had just been born when I had to leave the family to join up with England for that autumn series with New Zealand, Australia and South Africa. That left Amanda with much to cope with alone.

I had been at the birth of our other two children, so imagine my disappointment at not being with Amanda when she needed me most. I had travelled to Glasgow to play for Sale in a European fixture, but only after checking that Amanda felt no immediate symptoms. The next day, however, Amanda called to say the birth was imminent. Fortunately, Lynne was there. Jim Mallinder, a family man himself, let me head for home to be with Amanda. That was thoughtful. I had gone to Scotland in my own car in case I needed to go home and I was on course to get to the hospital on time when a road accident delayed me, just minutes from the hospital. When I finally arrived, I was twenty-five minutes too late to witness Joseph's entry into this world.

Amanda had always liked the name Joseph, and Cameron had chosen it when he told Amanda he wanted a baby brother.

Amanda suggested to Cameron that he pray for God to send him a brother, and then they opened the Bible at random to read it together, and it fell open to a passage about Joseph. Very soon after that, Amanda discovered she was expecting a baby.

Cameron and Jemimah were delighted when they arrived at the hospital and found out they had a baby brother. It was a great blessing to see a young boy's faith in God grow through answered prayer.

Amanda sees me for who I am, not for the person I am perceived to be on a rugby pitch. She doesn't watch much television or buy newspapers. We have to work at keeping our family functioning as it needs to, despite the pressure. She finds there are some very kind and understanding people involved in rugby union. Apart from my relationship with God, my family is the most important aspect of my life and I know they have had to take a back seat at times. I am grateful that I have been able to make a life for us all by playing rugby, but I understand that it won't last forever.

In a way, going to train is no different from going to the office. It's my job and there is a lot of hard work to be done. Some days are good, some days are better than that, and some days I don't feel like getting out of bed in the morning. After a dozen years as a professional, and almost ten years as an international in both codes, the strain takes its toll. When I came back from the three-Test autumn series, I spoke with Sale captain Bryan Redpath, a Scotland international, and we couldn't believe how tired we were after a tough three weeks in camp. I was shattered and carrying some niggling injuries. That's the reality behind the glamour. That's the man families get to see close-up. There will come a time when this is all over and you'll expect your family just to be there. The need to be at your peak each match day is demanding mentally and physically. I am not complaining, it's just how it is. It's hard to switch off and come home and be a nice husband and father.

Club rugby's demanding enough, but in a year such as 2003 with the World Cup at the end of it, you can assume that you will be away from home for another six months.

In a routine week with Sale, if we play at home on a Friday night, we are back in to the club the next morning for a recovery session. That might consist of doing some cardiovascular work and some swimming, and getting hot and cold treatment to circulate the blood and get rid of all the toxins. Sunday is a day off. Monday includes a weight session in the morning, followed by a debrief of the game we played on Friday with a run-through of the video film. Afterwards, we have a rugby session. Tuesday, we have a sprint session at 10 a.m., followed by a rugby session that incorporates some defence, some ball handling and some team work. At 3 p.m. fitness coach Marty Hulme runs an extra session for anyone he feels needs to do a bit more. On Wednesday, it's more rugby work at a ground near Manchester United's training centre. Lunch is followed by a weights session, then there is hydrotherapy with hot and cold treatment. Daytime on Thursday is free, but we come in early evening for the captain's run-through, a forty-minute briefing. On Friday, we meet around 6.15 p.m. for an 8 p.m. kick-off.

I've probably already played more games – around thirty-five a season – than most people play in a career. I've missed about ten in the last eight years due to injury. The worst injury I sustained happened back in 1993, just after I'd made my debut for the Great Britain rugby league team against New Zealand.

That was when I dislocated my elbow and couldn't play for six weeks. If I stay fit and healthy, I could have another four years left at the top level. I will assess my future when my contract comes to an end in 2005.

Life is a constant reappraisal. I often talk about it with Maurice Barratt, a good friend who, in recent years, has come to our house on most Tuesday evenings to study the Bible with a group of us. Maurice has said that, in his view, God often lets people like me use their drive and ego to make themselves the best and then, when they get to be the best, he shows us that we are nothing.

I met Maurice in Wigan, when he was preaching at a church in Hindley Green. His subject was success and failure, and because he had been an international gymnast, he used the theme of sportsmen. The winning of a gold medal can't glorify God, he reasoned, you could still be a womaniser or a drunk. It's character that counts, not pride in your achievements. He was knocking Christian sportsmen who shouted about their faith.

Apparently, at the end of the meeting, someone asked him, 'Did you preach that because Jason was there?'

'Who's Jason?' he said. Maurice doesn't follow rugby so he was none the wiser when he was told.

When we moved to Sale, we got to know him better. We went to listen to him and then he started to come to the house. I don't get to church very often and Maurice said he was prepared to come round. He invited us to get a few people together if we wanted. We welcomed this opportunity. Gradually, I told him about my past.

This is how he sees it:

What I have found is that Jason wants to know himself. This is quite unusual really, especially from Christians. They are taught to be hypocrites from the moment they enter the church, which is sad. And yet Jason really wants to be honest. You don't expect that of someone of his status. He listens, he takes a few notes. He will latch on to something and put it into practice in his life. For example, I remember saying that as Christians in today's world, it is not enough to act in business in a legal way alone. It might be all right, but what does that count for if your dealings might also be immoral. Stealing off the government by use of a tax loophole is still stealing off the government. God is not interested in legalities. He's interested in morals. Jason took this to heart and altered his attitude and approach to business. I was surprised. His decision was rare, even for a Christian.

It does me good to talk to him. I go to his home on a Tuesday and the group is small. The most we have had is a dozen. It's free. I am not trying to build a church. I teach principles not doctrine. I am coming from my own searchings, from hating hypocrisy and trying to get some reality. I realise a lot of the Church won't like that. My message is clear. I say, 'Think what I am saying, don't just accept it. Study it, check with your Bible.' There is no problem if people disagree.

I suppose I have been an influence in Jason's life, but I'd hate to be thought of as some sort of guru who gave him advice on everything from his marriage to his business. He sometimes talks to me about his plans, but he very much has a mind of his own. He is not as laid back as people might assume. He has strong views and I don't think he is easily led. I know some of his many pressures as a sportsman, father and businessman. We talk about that. I think he is open with me. I can relate to the pressures on him. Often I am out late preaching and I have a wife and three young children, and when I am at home I am running the media ministry.

I use the media to get the teaching out, writing books and making audio and visual teaching tapes.

The fact is Jason hasn't belonged to a church for some years after he became unhappy with where he and Amanda were worshipping. I do believe you need fellowship with like-minded people, so a house group is ideal for someone in Jason's situation. The church actually is people. People can't go to church. They are the church. We have strange ideas that the church is to do with buildings and candles, but the truth is wherever you meet with Christians, that is the church. Instead of an organisation it's an organism, a living body of people.

It's not always easy to go to church – sometimes I am away from home on Sunday mornings – but more than that, it is hard to find a church that we are comfortable with. Anyway, we want our relationship to be right with God and that is not about sitting in a pew every Sunday.

I pray to God now in everything I do, and try to live my life by following the gospels. I don't want to create a picture of being a Bible carrier because I'm not. I just want to have the right attitude.

I get paid to do a job and just as I'd want somebody to work hard if I hired them to do some plumbing or building, I do the same for those who are paying me. I realise there is a big responsibility on me. The more time passes, the more committed I am to what I do. Like it or not, I am a role model. I'm in a position where through rugby and through my Christian beliefs, my behaviour may affect somebody who comes from a totally different background from me. You just don't know how many people are watching you, and are influenced by what is acceptable to you. I want people to see you don't have to follow the crowd. Don't get me wrong, sometimes it is hard going against the grain, but I once heard someone suggest, 'It's the dead fish that go with the flow.'

On journeys to away matches, I might move to sit next to Marty at the front of the bus, if a video's running that I prefer not to see, for instance. I wouldn't dream of demanding that it be switched off. We're not a wild bunch, but the boys might want to put on 'Hannibal', and that's the time for a cup of coffee and a chat with Marty.

As I've mentioned, our television at home is mainly used for playing the children's videos. I do consider most of what is shown on television to be a waste of time. I also think that much of it is a corrupting influence. Adverts on television, as well as in magazines or on billboards, use sex to sell products, because it works. It's natural for a man to desire a woman and the advertising industry uses this in a corrupt way. I'd rather not let that stuff into my house because it has no benefit to us. We monitor everything our children watch, including their videos.

So much on television is trying to de-sensitise us. Why don't we let our children have their childhood? So much of what we are presented with is bad, with fighting, killing and lust. They will see all that soon enough whether we like it or not; we must face the fact that there is no escape from it. But not yet – we want to bring them up in a Godly way, to respect other people.

It would be easy to sit back and let them have the television remote so they could watch whatever they wanted, just as it would be easy for us to send them to school, giving Amanda more time for herself. We sent Cameron to an independent Christian school for a year. The people there were really nice, but it didn't work out. We felt we were hardly seeing him – and

Cameron complained that he wasn't seeing his sister because he was at school all day. Now Amanda teaches Cameron at home.

When Amanda first mentioned educating Cameron at home, I didn't think it was for us. I'd never heard of home schooling and it seemed an extreme path. But Amanda convinced me that the benefits would be enormous, not only for Cameron but also for Jemimah and for us as parents. We would have greater input. If we were to leave our children to society to bring up, what values would they have?

It's a choice, isn't it? I'm not saying that it's right for everyone, but we think it is right for us. Amanda agrees that children are exposed to corrupting influences too young. This is how she puts it:

> I want them to be strong enough to know what they think and what they believe before they are exposed to having to make decisions. I want them to be protected from peer pressure, which is so powerful. I have a curriculum to teach from and we continually re-evaluate our home school approach in order to tailor it to Cameron and us as a family, and also to give him as interesting and varied an education as possible, as well as nurturing in him good character. We use some of the ACE curriculum – Accelerated Christian Education – from the United States, but one of the disadvantages is that it is a bit Americanised. Still, it is not difficult to tell Cameron that we say autumn and not fall.
>
> Cameron is not isolated. Jason didn't start to play rugby until he was ten, and Cameron has been to the Preston Grasshoppers. He was not impressed because it was played as a non-contact sport for his age group. To Cameron, rugby is boring without being able to tackle!

Ultimately, we have to trust God. He knows the reasons we are doing this. I was very affected by peer pressure and I don't want my children to go down the same road I did. I know what happened to me. I can't afford to stand back and let that happen because they are my children and I love them. I was concerned at the beginning about them not socialising, but the reality is that Cameron's inhibitions have gone, barriers have come down. If you think about it, it's an artificial situation to have the same aged people together with you all the time. It's far more normal for him to interact with people on different levels, adults and children.

Cameron has a desk in the dining room and he works better if we stick to a disciplined routine. After that, he is free to go on his computer or play with his Lego or other educational toys. An added plus point is that he has a strong bond with his sister. He definitely missed her when he went to school for a year when he was five. After that first year, we saw that Cameron going to school did not work for us as a family. I think the world would be a better place if the emphasis was placed on encouraging young people to have better character and attitude, rather than the system we have where, to my mind, education is being solely driven by academic performance. It took a while before Jason was convinced that this would be right for us as a family.

Cameron is happy, I can see that. He is getting a one-on-one education, which he would not get at school. Part of the reason for my lack of achievement at school is that I was lost in a classroom of thirty-five children. How does a teacher get round to everyone? If you are weak in an area – which obviously I was – they might not always know, especially if you are as shy as I was. They could see from marking my books that I was not doing very well, but they were not able to spend the time with me that I needed. Who knows the child best, teacher or parent?

Home schooling is not the norm, but nor is it extreme. We faced pressures from family and friends who feared Cameron could be isolated, but Amanda meets other home schoolers and they go out as a group for the day. Another bonus is that if I go away for rugby, it is feasible for the family to come with me. If the children were in school that would be disruptive. Cameron loves being at home with his mum, his sister and now his baby brother. He's being brought up with principles. What more could we want? I see my other son Lewis every week and we do things together as a family. Lewis and the other children are good friends and I believe I've been able to maintain a father–son relationship with him. I have provided for him from the beginning and when Lewis is with us he is part of the family, which is how it should be. He is a football fan – something I am not – and mad keen to see Manchester United. I'm planning to take him to see them play.

People often think that because of my devotion to Christianity, my life must be restricted, but I feel freer now than I have ever done. I can say yes or no – I couldn't say no before. Things are not always as they seem. I am strong enough to do what I feel is right, no matter who is asking. If I want to sit at home and drink six pints of beer I can. It's just that I no longer have the need to do that. It is of no benefit to me. It is only since becoming a Christian that I realise how bound I was before.

We don't keep Christmas, partly because Jesus was not born on 25 December. Christ's birth is a reason to be thankful – although I am rather more thankful that Christ died for my sins and rose again – but I don't want to place all the emphasis on that one day. We have peace in our house on 25 December, like any other day. We try to be sensitive to family and friends, but it is difficult and they may not understand why we don't celebrate Christmas any more. Our children have many wonderful things, but we want them to understand that there are more important factors in life than being materialistic.

I certainly haven't got everything right and there are areas where I fall down. I am caring for my family in the way I think is best. I play rugby and I get well paid. In addition, I am fortunate to have endorsement contracts with Puma, Marks and Spencer, where I promote the View From range, Lloyds TSB, Cadbury chocolate, the Powerade energy drink company, Tissot watches and Land Rover. I am careful about the companies I deal with – I like to know a bit about them before signing up. I am fortunate to have built good relationships with the companies that I do represent. I feel comfortable with my commercial portfolio because I have responsibilities as a father, husband and provider. I have a short career and it would be negligent of me not to insure my family's future. It is sometimes a juggling act to keep everyone happy, but I have great assistance from Sian Masterton from Octagon, who looks after my portfolio and keeps me on my toes. We work well together. For instance, she finds out in advance what photographs are liable to be taken on a corporate day. She knows I will not compromise myself for any photo shoot.

As well as Sian, Dave Swanton at Sale tries to keep my diary in some kind of order. Swanny's son Dan is also a help – although I did ask him to take down the pictures of Kylie Minogue that he had above his desk in his dad's office in the PortaKabins that constitute the administrative suite at Sale. Dan makes sure that for home games I have always signed a hundred photos so I can just give them out. That way I get to eat with the other boys.

Swanny deals with my correspondence. I always want to answer every letter personally and do everything that's asked of me. Unfortunately that's not possible, but I do make sure I reply to the many people who write to me at the club about my Christianity. In fact, I have been known to ring some of them up. That shocks them, I can tell you.

We get a lot of requests from schools for coaching visits, but it's hard to fit in going to places that are too far afield, such as Newquay. Swanny was funny about one place in Lytham St Anne's. The school had entered a sevens tournament and they wanted me on the Wednesday after my England debut against Italy. I said we'd do it in their lunch hour. Swanny said, 'Robbo, it's Blackpool. That's fifty-five miles away.' I said, 'So what?' and off we went, fifty-five miles there and fifty-five miles back to coach them in their dinner hour. I'd promised, you see.

Swanny has a show on BBC Radio Lancashire and I'm always asking for requests to be played – the Temptations, Otis Redding, Lionel Richie. He teases me about being tight, getting records played for Amanda instead of buying her presents. Swanny is generous with his time, doing some fund-raising for a multiple sclerosis charity. He was helping with an auction in Wigan one time, and I donated my kit from my last-ever rugby league game, the Grand Final in 2000. I didn't see much point in keeping it in the loft when it could be put to better use. I thought it might raise a hundred quid or so, but the organisers held it back for a bigger night. Last I heard, there had been a bid of £1,500 – for rugby kit!

In writing this book, I have had to confront my life in full for the first time. I have taken hard stock and I have come to understand that in order to move forwards, sometimes you need to look back. I had been hiding from some of my past because it was easier to pretend that it had never happened. I have had to recognise that.

Looking back at how I was makes me want to look forward to the future. In life, you make a lot of mistakes, and I have made more than my share. That is not the crime, though. The real crime would be if you failed to learn from them. I believe I have learned and I believe I have got stronger in the process.

When I am finished with rugby, I hope to do something that has a good purpose. I don't know what. For the present, I am still struggling with myself. There are things in me that nobody else sees, things that I really don't like to own up to. That's life. You have your ups and downs, and success or failure is judged by the way that you deal with them.

As a family we have Christ. Without Christ we wouldn't have a family. It's a miracle that we are together. What's happened has happened because God wanted it to happen.

As a final reflection on life's journey to this point, I am much happier with Jason Robinson now than the Jason Robinson before 1995. At the same time, I am looking forward to meeting Jason Robinson in ten years from now.

INDEX